24/7 Flow

Thrive Around the Clock

by

Paula Petry, PhD

and

Leigh Kapps, PhD

Ubiquity
University
Publishing

Ubiquity University
Publishing

ISBN: 978-1-963036-03-9

paulapetry.com

kappstone.com

Front cover design and illustration by Brandon Frazier.

Book design and layout by Jon Cheetham Design Ltd.

joncdesign.co.uk

Dedication

To Humanity's Awakened Destiny.

Table of Contents

About the Authors

Leigh Kapps, PhD

Leigh is a trained music therapist with a doctoral degree in Education and Administration from the University of Miami. She was the COO of United Community Options of South Florida (Former United Cerebral Palsy) for 42 years.

She began a spiritual quest early in life at the age of 9 when her father died. She sought answers to life's meaningful questions regarding where her father went and the meaning of life. She found her teacher at the age of 22 and spent 14 years studying with her, fully embracing her teachings.

With Leigh's background in music, healing, and hypnotherapy she develops workshops and retreats and works one-to-one with individuals. Her work is a joyful path filled with meaning and connection to one's higher self.

Her website is **kappstone.com**

Paula Petry, PhD

Paula guides personal transformation with a diverse background spanning academia and holistic healing. Departing from conventional academia after a decade at the University of Miami's medical school, Paula sought deeper self-connection, catalyzed by personal tragedy – the loss of her daughter. Embarking on a profound journey of self-discovery and healing led her to explore realms beyond the tangible, delving into the mysteries of consciousness and the afterlife. She distilled her insights into her first book, her memoir, *"A Mother's Courage to Awaken."*

As keynote speaker, author, and practitioner, Paula shares her wisdom through story and science, illuminating the interconnectedness of all life. Her transformative work empowers individuals to align with their inner truth and transcend adversity.

For inquiries and to learn about her *Parenting Between Worlds©*, write to **paula@paulapetry.com**, or visit her website at **paulapetry.com**.

Preface

Dear Reader,

Our journey together as authors began from a common ground – Paula and Leigh, two individuals navigating the twists and turns of life in the vibrant city of Miami, Florida.

At the time, we were both working in the field of disability. Leigh, an administrator, and Paula, a devoted parent to a child with a disability, who served as a passionate advocate for her and other children. Ironically, we often found ourselves on opposite sides of the 'negotiations table,' each pursuing our roles in the realm of disability services. Little did we know that, years later, we would uncover a golden thread that would weave our paths together in profound ways.

Our golden thread came in the form of loss. The type of loss that creates an emptiness that's too vast to be filled with the life known before. Both Paula and Leigh have faced such losses. Leigh lost her father when she was only 9, and Paula's daughter, Alexandra, passed away at the age of 12, a loss that left her grieving for many years.

We each sought meaning and answers to these unexpected tragedies in different ways. Traditional supports played a role in our journeys, but they didn't fully answer our questions. Paula explored psychoanalysis and belonged to a Methodist Church. Leigh was raised Catholic but attended every religious denomination in her small town after her father's death, always leaving with a sense that something important remained unresolved.

In time, both of us found our answers. Paula's colleague handed her the book Courageous Dreaming, introducing her to shamanic energy medicine, a bridge between the spiritual and physical worlds, guiding energy for healing purposes. Leigh found her answers when she attended a spiritual event announced on a poster at her college campus, where her future mentor sat down next to her. Through our persistent seeking, and by engaging in the very practices we share with you here, we created lives more fulfilling than we could have imagined.

In these pages, we share our experiences, offering insights into how awakening and wellness practices work together, creating a holistic approach to life. Throughout, we explain the what and why of a practice because we know it makes the how easier to do. This happens because giving meaning to what you're doing makes it work better.

This book isn't a strict set of rules. We know there are infinite possibilities for your path to greater joy and flow. It is rather a friend, an initial guide on your personal journey toward balance and a sense of well-being, supported by practices that create flow in your life.

As you dive into the upcoming chapters, see the book as an invitation to explore your own self. Find the potential in your breath, the calm in music, and the transformative power when your inner and outer worlds align.

May this book inspire you, guide you in uncertain moments, and spark positive changes in your life. Let these pages unfold not just as a story but as a roadmap to awakening and wellness – a celebration of the vibrant symphony of your life.

Warmly and purposefully,

Paula Petry and Leigh Kapps

Endorsements

"24/7 Flow: Thrive Around the Clock is a practical guide to living a conscious life. Paula and Leigh have woven together easy to do techniques with examples of how these have improved their lives and those of their clients. For those readers who are seeking more meaningful lives in a busy and chaotic world, this is the book for you.

"It has inspired me to live day by day instead of worrying about the past or the future. This easy-to-read book can transform your life!"

Paula Matthew, CSJ

"Now more than ever, families who have a child with a disability need this book to navigate the unique challenges they face. Paula and Leigh's toolkit about ways to reduce the effects of stress offers invaluable support for parents.

"It is a beacon of hope, illuminating a path toward increased resiliency."

Lori Fahey, CEO,
The Family Cafe

"Paula and Leigh have written a gem of a book that can be revisited on multiple occasions.

"Combining practical techniques, accessible theory and personal examples, it provides you with a concise, effective and self-empowering manual for living a present, flowing and fulfilling life."

Luigi Sciambarella, Board Member,
Monroe Institute

"To live in flow is to experience life at its best. Currently, both as a society and as individuals, we find ourselves out of flow – constantly chasing, distracted, and lost.

"This book offers powerful, actionable techniques grounded in scientific research that help the reader achieve more frequent states of flow. It's an important read for anyone seeking to infuse their life with greater ease and joy."

Hannah Power, Performance Coach
and Host of Flow, the Podcast

"24/7 Flow is a beacon of wisdom in a chaotic world. Paula and Leigh's book is a lifeline, offering practical techniques, profound insights, and personal anecdotes that resonate deeply.

"It embodies the principles of flow and presence in everyday life. Whether you're navigating the challenges of daily existence or seeking deeper meaning, this book serves as a guiding light, illuminating the path to more joy and love in your life"

Paris Ackrill, Director and Co-Founder,
Avalon Wellbeing Centre, Broughton Sanctuary

"Sophisticated spiritual thinkers and writers, Paula and Leigh's depth of empathy and natural skills in personal inquiry make them true guides – sensing beyond the evident.

"Their words carry layers of meaning and compassion, holding space for much more than the reader's immediate quest. Residing in a higher awareness, they speak directly to the totality of being human, inviting in wisdom and grace as the companions for authentic self-discovery."

Kirsty Lucinda Allan, Founder, The IF Crowd

Acknowledgements

The journey of crafting this book has been one of profound growth and gratitude. We owe immense thanks to those who supported us every step of the way.

First and foremost, our deepest gratitude to our spiritual guides, mentors, and teachers whose steadfast support behind the scenes has enriched our lives and paved the path for us to bring this book to fruition.

A special acknowledgment goes to Cathleen O'Connor, our editor, whose invaluable direction and insightful advice shaped the manuscript into its final form. We are equally appreciative of her meticulous edits and unwavering commitment to maintaining the coherence of our work. Our heartfelt thanks also extend to Brandon Frazier, the artist whose talent transformed our vision into a striking book cover.

We are profoundly grateful to Ubiquity University for their unwavering faith in our work and dedication to realizing our vision. To Broughton Sanctuary for their many contributions. We extend our sincere appreciation to The Family Café Inc. for their trust in our mission and their tireless efforts to empower families with children with disabilities, alleviating the impacts of stress in their lives.

To our readers, we extend our deepest gratitude for your interest. It is our sincere hope that this book proves to be a valuable resource for you. Your engagement with its tools and processes is the ultimate reward for our efforts.

Lastly, we express heartfelt gratitude to each other for being exceptional co-authors and steadfast partners. Your expertise, collaboration, and friendship have made this endeavor both rewarding and unforgettable.

With profound appreciation,

Paula and Leigh

Introduction

You are invited to embark on a journey, one in which you will learn the secrets of crafting a life that flows smoothly every day. This adventure will take you into the interesting space where continuous flow meets wellness practices and the discovery of your inner self.

What lies beyond our physical selves is a cohesive interconnecting field of energy, and the ease and flow with which your life unfolds is influenced by your understanding and interaction with the powerful forces embedded in this field.

While the healing techniques offered here are accessible to everyone, their power lies in giving you access to the healing love that exists within this field and within yourself. As you connect with this field, you gently shift towards an awakened life that flows easily 24/7.

Awakening often comes out of sorrow. Yet, even in your darkest hours following such loss, you are never alone, the universe is supportive, and there is life after life.

The daily rituals, diverse practices, and universal truths presented within these pages will profoundly enrich your life. They serve as pillars that will support your ongoing journey. Most importantly, they will give you the information and motivation to formulate your 'around the clock' flow schedule so you can awaken to a life that flows with ease.

Think of this book as a toolkit for mind, heart, body and spirit. In this toolkit are practices that you may do now, and there are practices that may be new to you. What makes this book unique is the marriage of science and spirituality.

By understanding the miraculous organism that is your human body, the practices and why they work become clearer. You may find yourself drawn to a particular practice and not others. That is fine. Allow your intuition to guide you as you read and work with the concept of 24/7 flow. Each chapter offers one specific technique from your toolkit that is transformative.

The book is organized to take you into a day. Yet the techniques offered expand beyond the boundaries of any one day. They are life techniques to be drawn on, so you can create your unique interpretation of 24/7 flow that works for you.

As you read Chapter One, you'll get to know the journeys of the authors and how each came to the healing state of flow. Start your relationship with the book there, and take the self-assessment in Chapter One – as that will confirm for you how this book and this toolkit might speak to your life today.

Then delve into Chapter Two and rethink how your usual day begins.

Every day is a new beginning, and what you make of that beginning can set the tone for your experience of the entire day. Explore each chapter and incorporate what resonates with you at this point in your life. Choose what calls to you. This book is a toolkit that can be used in part or whole.

Approach the book as a woven tapestry of threads combining daily practices, stories that inspire, activities, and the transformative strength found in being brave beyond the usual ideas of health. The tools are provided but it is you, and only you, who can create your personal blueprint for a life of flow and ease.

The journey begins.

Chapter One :
Defining Flow

"When you love someone, the best thing you can offer is your presence. How can you love if you are not there?"

Thich Nhat Hanh

How much of your day do you spend not there?

Do you find yourself so busy that your body hurts, your heart numbs, and your mind is chatter-central? If you were an artist, and you are, the painting you would paint of your most favorite scene would have ample use of what is called 'white' space where the eye can not only rest but must do so to fully appreciate the vibrancy of the composition and colors.

When you are overextended or overly busy, your life lacks the very white space you need to reflect, rest and recalibrate self. It is the beauty of that white space that provides flow, that experience of full presence, of being fully engaged whether in a conversation, walking in nature or delving into a creative pursuit.

Flow is when your awareness and your experience seem synchronized, where time is no longer a limited taskmaster but elastic, and where body and mind are effortlessly one.

Is it possible to be in flow, 24/7?

It is, and this book provides a roadmap for you to follow, a roadmap that we developed through our own painful experiences. A roadmap that we have seen work not only in our own lives but with hundreds of clients, several of whom you will meet on these pages.

Leigh's Story

I lost my beloved father at the tender age of 9 and can still conjure up the feelings of shock and disbelief that I experienced when the school principal called me out of my classroom to be with my mother, who gave me the devastating news.

I could not understand how he could be here one minute and gone the next. It made me question my faith in God. Just as I was settling into a new normalcy, my mother remarried a man with two children of his own.

My stepfather had no interest in his children or in me. I was left to fend for myself, with two children who were strangers. I felt unloved and abandoned by my mother. I hated my stepfather, became more and more sullen and depressed, and my grades started to slip.

My 'escape' to college gave me the opportunity to make wonderful life-long friends, but I was unhappy and could not escape the hate in my heart for the stepfather who I saw as the reason for my pain.

When I was 22, I met the woman who became my teacher, and through working with her I learned to take responsibility for my own life and stop blaming others, especially my stepfather. I learned to connect with the spark of divinity that was within him and began a practice in earnest to heal the pain from this relationship. Even though he knew nothing of my practice our relationship began to heal.

When he was on his deathbed, I was able to tell him that I forgave him for how he had treated me, and I apologized for how sullen and unreachable I had been. He was near death with Alzheimer's at that time, but his daughter told me that after she put the phone to his ear, and I spoke with him, that he relaxed and died peacefully.

Having that hate in my heart interrupted the natural flow of my life resulting in some health issues and problems in relationships. Although the practice of connecting to my stepfather's divinity proved to affect him and our relationship in a positive way, it was not the most important outcome.

The heart-centered practice helped me create a better life for myself. It brought me into that sacred space of flow. My early losses and my open heart led me to dedicate my professional career to helping people with disabilities and their families to have quality lives. I have seen how the techniques you'll experience in this book transform lives.

They transformed mine and I hope they do the same for you.

Paula's Story

I was pregnant and living with my husband, Jaime, in the Dominican Republic when my beautiful daughter, Alex, was born. She was immediately taken away and placed in an incubator. I fell into a troubled sleep, not knowing what was wrong.

That evening, two doctors entered my stark hospital room. Our pediatrician and a neurosurgeon delivered the devastating news: my daughter had a severe form of spina bifida. She would be unable to walk, use her bladder and bowels, and would have 'mental retardation', the term at the time.

Overwhelmed with sadness and shock, Jaime and I could only nod in response to their explanations. That night, alone in my hospital room, I began to have seizures. In the morning, I was diagnosed with eclampsia, a fatal condition when left untreated.

The doctors communicated mostly through my husband. Their recommendation was to leave our daughter in the hospital; within a short time she would die of a brain infection. Everyone seemed to agree with the physicians.

Looking back, I have to say that one of the most courageous decisions I ever made was to bring my daughter home from the hospital. Courage is needed when there is a misalignment between one's mind and one's heart, as it requires a sacrifice in some form.

But, when we live aligned, our heart, mind and soul yoked together, doors fly open, synchronicities happen.

That is exactly what happened over the next twelve years, although my grief and sadness and old ways of thinking prevented me from realizing it, but I was living in divine flow. We had moved to Miami, had our son, and I worked as a passionate advocate for my daughter and other children with disabilities throughout the state of Florida.

My prominent position at the university's medical school, teaching future pediatricians about the family's perspective was rewarding. I felt I had a purpose-driven life and envisioned traveling with my daughter sharing our story and inspiring others. It was not to be. My beautiful Alex died at age twelve.

The horrific pain from the loss of a child can't ever be captured on the page. It is a one-foot-in-front-of-the-next experience. People often ask me, what got me to the other side of grief? It is never one thing.

My church community was essential early on. My son and I were at the United Methodist church three times a week. We both had a therapist and I saw a psychiatrist for anti-anxiety medication and an anti-depressant. Although we slowly felt better, there was a large part of the both of us that went unhealed. Life moved us forward, but I was stuck in my grief.

In 2007, my deepest healing began. I resigned my position and undertook a year-long study of shamanic energy medicine.

My soul was ready to shift gears, my academic days needed to come to an end. I was to embark upon a more important journey, an inward one, where the deep peace I was longing for could be found. Before long I was seeing clients, helping them connect with their departed loved ones, giving shamanic energy sessions, removing heavy energies from their auric field.

The passion and enthusiasm I once had returned. For the first time, I had a sense of dominion over my own life. I had stepped into flow at a new level. I now use the techniques you will experience here in my own life and with clients, with amazing results. The journey lies before you. It is one I hope you will take.

Self-Assessment

Now that you've gotten to meet your co-authors, it is time for you to consider the state of your own life. This abbreviated self-assessment is designed to help you reflect on your inner life and begin to identify aspects of yourself you would like to strengthen or heal. The full questionnaire is available at **24-7flow.com**. Take it for immediate feedback when you have time.

For the moment, suspend doubt and answer as honestly as you can. Your life is wholly your own, not to be compared with anyone else's. Find a quiet space where you will not be interrupted and carefully consider each item. After, you will be guided through a future visioning process – where you experience the joy that flow brings.

As you work through this book, you'll connect with your inner life in new and empowering ways.

The six check boxes identify your level of agreement with the statement. If you very strongly disagree, check the leftmost box. If you very strongly agree, check the rightmost box. The scale shown here corresponds to the six boxes in the survey.

	STATEMENT	A	B	C	D	E	F
1	I see ordinary things as extraordinary						
2	I feel hopeful						
3	I feel in control of worrisome thoughts						
4	I feel in control of anxious feelings						
5	I feel positive about things						
6	There's something to look forward to						
7	I feel worthy as a person						
8	I feel confident in my decisions						
9	I feel fate is on my side						
10	I feel free to choose what my life is going to be like						

SCALE:

A = Very Strongly Disagree

B = Strongly Disagree

C = Disagree

D = Agree

E = Strongly Agree

F = Very Strongly Agree

While the full on-line *Joyful Living* questionnaire reflects your overall level of joy, this subset of questions can also give you valuable insights.

Take a moment to think about the items you scored lower on compared to others. Maybe you are struggling with worthiness or lack of luster in your life. Worry is perhaps weighing heavily on you. Choose two or three of these low-scoring items and set an intention to work on improving these areas over the next three months, using the tools you'll choose from your toolkit.

Remember, your full Joyful Living assessment with your digital score and interpretation is at **24-7flow.com**.

Eileen's Story

Eileen was unhappy and in pain. She was getting more and more upset with her husband.

As he was aging, he became dissatisfied with his life, feeling angry, useless, and bored. Eileen could not understand why she was not enough for him, and she began to turn this feeling into a hatred for him and what her life had become. He wanted a dog, but she did not. For Christmas, their children gave them a puppy, thinking it would improve their lives.

The puppy was difficult to train, and her husband took no part in helping. This made her hatred grow to include the dog. She reached out to Leigh, recognizing she needed help because she did not want to hurt the innocent puppy. Leigh shared her stepfather's story and Eileen began to connect with her husband's heart divinity. Slowly, she began to move from hatred to compassion. She started cooking his favorite meals, watched TV shows with him and tried to help him find activities he might enjoy like playing cards or dominoes.

The dog was another story. He was trained but Eileen continued to resent the dog for the extra work he created for her. Soon, her husband began to slip into dementia and the dog was a tremendous comfort for him. When her husband would become agitated, and nothing would calm him down, the dog was his balm. Eileen began to feel gratitude for the comfort the dog provided. The last time Leigh spoke with her, she was content and filled with love, despite her husband's condition. She had stepped into flow.

EXERCISE

Now that you have a basic understanding of FLOW and have done a self-assessment, it's time to envision yourself in a future state of flow.

Let go of any pre-conceived ideas of what that might look like and just allow yourself to experience this visualization as it unfolds. You can also do this visualization as a guided meditation available at **24-7flow.com**.

As in all meditations, find a quiet space indoors or outdoors where you won't be interrupted. Sit comfortably or lie down and take a few deep breaths to settle your energy and prepare for going within.

1. Close your eyes and count backwards from 10-1, telling yourself with each number you are more and more relaxed. When you reach 1, visualize, feel or imagine that your focus drops to your heart.

2. From that heart-centered space, imagine what you want your future to look like – be as specific as possible. See yourself accomplishing what you want, noting how you feel, what you see, hear, sense and touch. The more you can make the visualization a rich sensory experience, the better. Sink into it and enjoy it.

3. Now, once you feel you are fully in the experience, anchor the feeling by putting the middle finger and thumb of each hand together. Take a deep breath.

4. Gently, through the breath, bring your awareness back up and, when you are ready, open your eyes.

When you want to experience that feeling of flow that you created in the visualization again, use your anchor of touching the middle fingers and thumbs of each hand together.

Use your anchor often throughout your day to bring you back to the state of being you want to create. Through consistent practice, you will more and more easily experience flow in all aspects of your life.

Chapter Two :
Attract Your Perfect Day

"How you start your day is how you live your day.
How you live your day is how you live your life."

Louise Hay

What do you do when you first wake up?

Do you open your eyes and give thanks for another day?

Do you begin the day with worrisome thoughts or an overwhelming to-do list?

Perhaps you get up and your attention goes to aches and pains in your body. Maybe you wake up after a restless night, tired and grumpy, and less than excited about the day ahead. A new morning has arrived for you, and how you greet that morning matters.

90% of people start their day by checking their phones (texts, email, social media, news).

When was the last time you felt exuberant about your life? You may be going through life focused on what you need to get done and coping with feeling overwhelmed with the pressures of daily life. You experience moments of joy in response to certain events, but if the joy you feel is generated by outside events, it is not sustainable. A reliance on others, the weather, or even the stock market for your emotional mood and capacity to feel joy only adds to emotional ups and downs.

Alternatively, the techniques to living in flow, once practiced daily, generate feelings of bliss that come from within and aren't dependent upon outside circumstances.

You can move your day in a positive direction by developing new perspectives through proactive thinking and feeling, thereby brightening your entire day, combating depression, and moving from autopilot to purposeful living.

Purposeful living is living a life in *flow*.

Starting the day with a positive outlook leads to naturally flowing into a more intentional day filled with uplifting thoughts and actions. But how do you do that?

By now, unless you've been on another planet, you've heard all about *The Secret* and may have tried to work with the first tool offered in your *Living in Flow Toolkit – The Law of Attraction*.

Skeptics of the law of attraction refer to it as new age mumbo jumbo. Actually, this concept dates all the way back to the first century AD or at least to ancient Egypt. Hermes Trismegistus, whose name is a merger of the Greek god Hermes and the Egyptian god Thoth, is the reported source of what are known as the seven hermetic principles, revealed in ancient texts rediscovered in the fifteenth century.

These texts contained writings on philosophy, medicine, astrology, alchemy, and the occult. Along with interest in culture, science and rationalism, the texts spread throughout the Renaissance, influencing the development of the Western World.

As Christianity and the power of the Catholic Church grew to dominate Europe, these principles ran counter to that of religion and were labeled heretical. The book, **The Secret,** and the resulting publicity, discussion and films, brought the hermetic principles to a modern world ready to embrace new ideas.

When you think of the Law of Attraction, you can think of the seven hermetic principles, ancient wisdom available today. And you can thank quantum physics for the ability to study and confirm these principles, especially the third principle that states that the universe is composed of matter, which vibrates at a certain rate, and that matter is just a physical form of energy.

What appears to be solid is in fact just another form of energy. Your body is not just physical tissues and bone, but swirling energy, and your energy interacts with everything around you. Even the space between yourself and the objects around you is teeming with energy.

The reason you cannot see this energy has to do with the microscopic size of the molecular structure of everything within and without you. It is beyond the capacity of your limited senses. You cannot see electrical energy or microwave radiation or radio or TV frequencies, but you know they exist because of the results they produce.

Everything emits a vibration. One station on the FM radio has a different frequency or vibration than another. One plant has a different vibration than another. Even the chair you are sitting on has a vibration. One vibration affects another.

This was first discovered with sound. When a note is struck or sung, a corresponding sound of the same pitch is elicited on a nearby instrument. Other types of resonance include mechanical, magnetic, electrical and atomic, to name a few.

If you are old enough, you might remember a 1970's commercial for Memorex cassettes. It featured soprano Ella Fitzgerald singing *How High the Moon* and shattering a wine glass. Most glasses resonate at a frequency of high C. Ella had a vast singing range, and when she reached the high C, it resonated with the glass and caused it to shatter.

It is one thing to accept that sound and other forms of energy can affect the environments around them, but it is another thing to accept that thoughts can affect your environment. Perhaps you've heard of the experiments of Dr Masaru Emoto, a Japanese scientist who extensively studied the effects that human thought can have on water. Specifically, he studied the scientific evidence of how the molecular structure in water can be transformed when it is exposed to human words, thoughts, sounds and intentions.

The results of years of research showed that positive thoughts led to changes in water crystals that made beautiful geometric shapes such as snowflakes, whereas negative thoughts generated fearful and distorted shapes. Your body is 75 percent water! What you think has the power to affect your body in the same way Emoto's research revealed how the crystals in water were impacted by thoughts.

Because of the work of quantum physicists and researchers like Emoto, thoughts can be considered energetic entities that vibrate at certain frequencies, capable of attracting similar frequencies. This disputes the common phrase that opposites attract. In actuality, like attracts like.

Positive thoughts attract positive experiences and negative thoughts attract negative experiences. However, thoughts alone are not enough. You may be unaware of the thoughts you have daily, as they most likely are running underneath your conscious mind, like a ticker tape on a stock market channel. Thoughts are connected to feelings. Feelings are the energy that creates the momentum to emit the vibrations in a powerful way. This is why if you just recite affirmations in a rote manner, you most likely won't see the results you desire.

Quantum physics has shown that you transmit brain frequencies into your environment and these frequencies are forms of energy. This theory states that thoughts equal energy, energy equals matter and thus thoughts equal matter.

The most basic of all your functions is breathing. Every time you breathe in and out, you engage in a process of giving and receiving with your environment. With each inhalation, you take in oxygen and nitrogen that keeps you alive, and with each exhalation, you expel carbon dioxide that nourishes all plant life. Thus, you are interacting with your world just by being alive!

Putting What You Know into Action

Many books and programs in recent years have oversimplified how the law of attraction works. Because of that, you might have tried and failed in manifesting what you want in your life. And what's been missing is the science which provides the necessary information for success.

How you interact with your environment is very complicated based on quantum physics. Without exception, what you give thought to is what you get, but you also match your feeling frequency with your thought.

You can think of yourself as a magnet, drawing to you what you are thinking and feeling. You have thousands of thoughts per day, so it is very difficult to monitor them, and make sure they are positive. Approximately 80% of these thoughts are negative. You also tend to have the same type of thoughts every day. The older you get the more you think the same thoughts. So, what can you do?

Rather than monitor your thoughts, pay attention to your feelings. These are your energy fuels that ensure your frequency matches what you desire. Oftentimes you may believe you are thinking in a positive way, but your body is telling you something different.

Maybe you think you are feeling very calm but when your blood pressure is taken, it is high, even though you do not normally have high blood pressure. Maybe you might have what is called white coat syndrome, where your blood pressure tests high when you go to see a doctor, and then settles back to normal after a few minutes.

This is a good example where you might have underlying anxiety (anxious thoughts and feelings) that don't arise in your conscious mind but still manifest in your body's blood pressure reading.

This is such a frequent occurrence that doctors often have patients record blood pressure at home to determine whether medication is needed.

Cathy's Story

Cathy believes firmly in natural alternatives unless pharmaceutical drugs are really needed. She has had surgeries that she recovered quickly from with the surgeon telling her that her rapid healing and successful surgery was due to the fact she was only on one medication, and it was one with minimal side effects.

But whenever Cathy went to see her primary physician her blood pressure was high.

After buying a good home monitor and having her doctor calibrate it to match the readings at her office, Cathy kept a log of her blood pressure several times throughout the day. Her doctor was still concerned, so she prescribed a very low dose of a blood pressure medication to see if it made a significant difference.

The second night she took the medication Cathy nearly passed out from low blood pressure. So, back to the doctor, more home monitoring, and a decision no blood pressure medication was needed. Instead, Cathy began working with the law of attraction, to dig out the fearful thoughts that might be causing her physical reactions at the doctor's office and to supplant those thoughts and feelings with the desired outcome of normal blood pressure.

She kept giving her body these positive messages and feelings several times a day and when she went to the doctor for her most recent visit, both she and her doctor were amazed that her blood pressure wasn't just in the normal range, it was in the normal range for someone much younger than she.

The synchronicity between your thoughts and feelings is of paramount importance in successfully manifesting your desires. Every thought and feeling you have will either strengthen or weaken you.

If you've been to a chiropractor lately, you may have experienced muscle testing, a method often used in that profession to determine what kind of supplements you might need to support your body. Muscle testing is also a good method to determine if you are having thoughts that strengthen you.

However, just like at the chiropractor, it should be done with a partner. To try it, hold your dominant arm out to the side of your body and have your partner press down and try to move your arm down. Say your name. When your arm is pressed, it should hold. Say an incorrect name, and your arm should drop when pressed even though you are resisting.

If you like this technique, try it with something you are working on for manifestation. Make a statement such as, *I am excited about getting the job of my dreams* and then muscle test.

If your arm holds, you know that your feelings are matching your words. If your arm falls, you know you have doubts about finding your dream job.

Opening Your Day

Now that you understand the importance of thoughts, feelings, and the law of attraction, it's time to put what you've learned into practice.

The beginning of the day is the perfect time to set in motion energies to attract your desires.

To do that you want to focus on what you want, not what you do not have. For example, if you concentrate on the fact that you do not have enough money, you'll only attract the same situation. Instead, you want to focus on the feeling of having money, enough for everything you want to have in your life.

As you do this, feel the satisfaction and joy of having the money you need. Remember, your feelings are the emotional energy that propels the thought into manifestation.

Lisa's Story

Lisa was going through her life on autopilot. She met a man, moved in with him, and they had two children. In her thirties, she was diagnosed with breast cancer. Her treatment was successful, and she was cancer free.

Despite this wake-up call, Lisa did not change her life in any significant way. Lisa and her live-in boyfriend were no longer a couple but continued to live together out of convenience.

Life moved on and her children grew older. Her son had a substance abuse problem. When he died of an overdose, Lisa finally realized her life had little meaning. She knew she needed to make some changes so she could move on from this tragedy.

A friend of hers introduced her to meditation. She began to meditate every day and slowly noticed she was dealing with her son's death better. She took the big step of leaving her boyfriend and moving out on her own.

Lisa began to feel like she deserved more in her life. She learned about manifestation and the Law of Attraction. She visualized finding the love of her life. She finally knew she deserved to be happy and fulfilled in a relationship.

She fully stepped into this new life as if it had already happened. It did not take long for this manifestation to become real.

She met the man of her dreams and married him in June of 2022 at the age of fifty-five years old. The wedding was held in the idyllic location of the Bahamas.

Once Lisa settled into her new marriage, she began to work on a new manifestation. She wanted to live in a house on the Treasure Coast of Florida off A1A, the highway that parallels the ocean. She shared this desire with her husband. He found a house on A1A but it was under contract. He told the agent he was willing to pay the asking price in cash. The contract fell through, and Lisa and her husband were able to purchase the house. She had become a master of the Law of Attraction!

Affirmations

Affirmations are a key component of the practice of the law of attraction, and often they are expressed in the present as I AM statements.

Because rote repetition will not produce results, you want to create affirmations that feel true to you and that you can express with both thought and feeling easily. The best ones will be ones you create for yourself but here are a few suggestions to get you started:

"I AM love and light. All is well"

"Today I take another step toward positive change."

"I AM at peace with my body, soul and mind."

Use your creativity to write specific affirmations such as these:

*"I know who I AM in the deepest part of my being.
It is up to me to create my life,"*

"With each new day and each breath I take, I have a fresh opportunity to live the life that I project with my thoughts and feelings."

"In the infinity of life, which is the eternal now, I AM perfect, whole and complete. I live in harmony and balance. Everything I need is there for me. There is an endless supply of love and light."

"I love myself and therefore, attract love. I think loving thoughts toward all people. I live in the now and see the world as a loving and positive place."

Leigh's Story

I have used affirmations my entire life. When I have a particular need, I go all out in using affirmations to manifest my desire. I have a general life mission statement in the form of an affirmation – *"I AM a source of Truth and Enlightenment for myself and others."*

I have typed this up and laminated it. I have put it in various places throughout my house. This has led me in all sorts of directions on my spiritual path and people who are interested in spiritual development have been drawn to me.

I decided my dog Oakley needed a companion. He has a lot of energy, and it is difficult for me to keep him occupied with enough exercise for him to be happy and healthy. I did not want to look for a purebred dog or make any effort in getting another one. I decided if a dog *"fell into my lap"*, I would consider it.

I wrote an affirmation that said, *"Oakley and I are so happy with our new puppy."* Within several weeks, I saw a post by a friend on Facebook who had two puppies. I called him and he said they were Yorkiepoos and were free to good homes.

As soon as Oakley saw the Yorkie puppy, he fell in love with him. We are a very happy family. I named the new puppy Bodhi, which means enlightenment.

EXERCISE

Make a plan for how you will begin your day tomorrow. Just plan for a single day. Think back to the questions at the beginning of this chapter and jot down what is true for you. Especially, jot down how you feel beginning your day the way you normally do.

What, if you had all the time in the world, would you change?

Often, you might think the issue is lack of time, but even with very limited time, you can start your day in a way that creates a new beginning. Try these simple steps:

- Before you get out of bed, take a few deep breaths.

- Notice how your body feels and express gratitude in your mind for your body's support during the night.

- Think about the energy you want to share with others for this single day.

- Say an affirmation you've created for yourself about what you hope to experience this day.

Louise Hay, who is quoted at the beginning of this chapter, used to begin her day, every day, with the simple affirmation, *Only Good Lies Before Me*.

With that affirmation, she set the energy for her day, regardless of what occurred. Affirmations are not to be considered something to say only once. If you want to work with affirmations, repeat the ones you set for yourself multiple times throughout the day. And place your affirmations in various places so you'll see them and be reminded.

If you are a beginner, work with one simple affirmation for something you desire (pick something that doesn't pose a life-changing result but that you would be happy to have).

Practice with that until you believe the process works.

Bill's Story

Bill wanted a new grill but didn't want to spend the money. He, instead, often repeated to himself, *"I love my new grill. I'm so happy I have it to cook on."*

He did this often throughout his day. On the third day a neighbor knocked on his door to ask him if he, by any chance, wanted a grill as he was getting rid of one.

It can truly be that simple!

How to write your own affirmations

1. Use positive words only – avoid negatives.

2. Think of a theme or need you have and write about manifesting it.

3. Write in the present tense.

4. State the result as fact, not a possibility.

5. Keep it authentic to your own voice and how you would speak.

Affirmations, and the other techniques you'll learn in this book, can be practiced within the scope of your everyday life. All that is asked of you is that you be willing to experiment. You are invited through these techniques to view the world as a positive place and yourself as a creative force within it.

"To bring anything into your life, imagine it is already there."

Author Richard Bach

You can think of the external world as a movie in which you are the director and writer, producing your own film, choosing the actors and the circumstances. Coming from this perspective can change your life.

You have a spiritual power filled with love and light.

Being mindfully conscious of how you begin your day and working with affirmations and the law of attraction to bring your life into alignment with your desires is deeply fulfilling. Your consciousness shifts into a higher frequency where the flow of life is effortless and joyful.

Chapter Three : Meditation

"The quieter you become the more you are able to hear."

Rumi

Do you meditate?

Have you tried to meditate but feel you never have enough time?

Do distracting thoughts that your busy brain summons keep you from sinking into the incredibly healing space of connectedness that meditation provides? If so, you are not alone.

Meditation is one of the most powerful tools in your flow toolkit. And there are many forms of meditation, but all share the aspect of focusing the mind on an object or a word to eliminate extraneous thoughts. If you're wondering about the origins of meditation, it was first mentioned in India in the Upanishads, sacred texts in Hinduism that are some of the oldest sacred writings in the world.

I have tried many forms of meditation through the years and have settled on a preferred method that I want to share with you here.

My form of meditation is called *"dropping into the heart."* In utero, the human heart is formed before the brain, so it seems to be the core aspect of self. Here is my process:

I begin the meditation by taking a few deep breaths to relax my body and to focus my mind. Then I move my attention to my face, which is where I operate from with my eyes open. Once I feel centered in this area, I move my attention down to my throat. I feel myself sliding down with intention so that I am viscerally in the throat area, feeling my head above me. Once I have this established, I then drop my focus down into my heart. As this is happening, I feel a movement inward toward the center of my chest, resting there.

This took practice before I could feel the shift in my awareness of where I was in the body. If you try it, you'll know you're in the process if you feel a deeper sense of relaxation as you move to each area, a sinking feeling as if you were going down in an elevator until you reach the heart. Once there, a sensation of centeredness occurs, allowing a sense of reaching a place within that is sacred. Just remaining there and bringing your mind back to the heart and sensation when it wanders can be a beautiful meditation.

Science alert! The heart has what is known as a toroidal nature. To understand what that means you have only to realize that the torus is one of the most fundamental shapes in nature. It is tube-shaped, like a donut, in its most basic form, and can be found in tree rings, butterfly/moth wings, red blood cells, tornadoes, and galaxy clusters.

In the heart's energy field, the torus spins in and out of the waves it creates, continuously flowing, creating an infinity shape. This energy is electromagnetic.

The heart is the most powerful source of this type of energy in the body, more powerful than the energy created by the brain. When the toroidal field of the heart is fully functioning and in balance, you are at your highest and best, creating a powerful energy field that promotes optimal health and attracts high vibrational frequencies from others.

When you drop into the heart you are entering the outermost toroidal field. Some refer to this as the sacred place in the heart. Once you drop and enter the outermost part, you can wait for an *"opening"* to occur to enter further into the inner toroidal field. This is accomplished by sensing this opening and then going through it. Immediately you will feel a further deepening of relaxation to the extent that the sensation of the body will begin to disappear, and you will feel suspended in a blissful state.

I was skeptical when I first heard about these two places in the heart. I had been doing the initial part of the meditation, going into the heart and feeling great peace. It was very relaxing, and I felt this was the purpose of my morning meditation. That daily practice allowed me to begin my day *"in the flow"* at a high frequency. I felt this helped me stay in a positive and upbeat mood and kept me from being dragged down by the stresses of the day.

However, going into the innermost part of my heart brought me to the core of my being. The word *"being"* is important because once this state is reached, the sense of individualization is gone.

The loss of bodily sensations leads to a feeling of being suspended in space. The blissful essence surrounds you and a connection of love with all things evolves. Even if this state lasts for only a minute or less, it can change your outlook on who you are and what life on earth means. If you do this exercise of dropping into the heart upon awakening, it can only take a few minutes. As you practice it, reaching the blissful state of connection can occur, maybe not every day, but often enough to make a difference in your life.

If you have not yet heard of the chakras, the concept of chakras originated in Hinduism, spread to other eastern belief systems, and came to the west in the teachings of H.P. Blavatsky of the Theosophical Society. There are seven major chakras (energy centers) located in the body from the base of the spine up to the top of the head.

They are energy focal points used in a variety of meditation practices. The heart chakra sits in the center of the body with three chakras above it and three below. It is a bridge between spiritual and earthly aspirations. It is the seat of illumed consciousness and the center of love and compassion for all of life.

Within the heart chakra is a divine spark from Source in all human beings. When you enter this sacred space through the heart drop meditation technique, you connect with this Source and feel the oneness of all sentient beings. This can become your own private meditation room. This is what St. Teresa of Avila referred to as *"The Interior Castle"*.

She wrote a book by this name, which describes the soul's progression through seven *"dwelling places"* until reaching the center. Remarkably, she wrote it during the Inquisition period in Spain. Despite all the chaos in the world, she was actually able to dive deeply into contemplation and reach the Truth within. She wrote it for her fellow Carmelite nuns.

In Matthew, chapter 6, verse 6, Jesus stated *"...when thou prayest, enter into thy closet and when thou hast shut the door, pray to thy Father in secret..."* He could have been referring to going into the heart. For Catholics, one of the sacred devotions to Jesus is the sacred heart and Mother Mary is celebrated through the Immaculate Heart.

In Hindu tradition, the devotee visualizes a jeweled island in the heart and sees himself before a beautiful altar where the guru is worshiped. Therefore, the heart is a very important area of the body across many religious traditions. It makes sense to devote some time each morning to reflect on *"going into the heart"* and exploring what benefits might be obtained by doing so.

Another layer of this practice is to focus on the concept of *"loving kindness"* from the Buddhist tradition, also known as *"metta"* in the Pali language. In Buddhist practice, this is a state of goodwill for all humankind that is cultivated by practice.

This is one of the central concepts of Buddhism as it is seen as an antidote for selfishness and suffering. Buddhists have an inherent desire for the happiness of others. His holiness, the Dalai Lama, has said this is his only reason for living.

I like to accompany my heart meditation practice with saying a short loving kindness prayer at either the beginning or the end. This is an example of a Buddhist-like prayer:

Loving Kindness

My heart swells with loving kindness.

May all beings everywhere, whether near or far,

Whether known to me or unknown be fulfilled.

May they be well.

May they be peaceful.

May they be free to co-create with the universe.

These phrases are often used in Buddhist prayers. The term *"co-create with the universe"* means that we can create our own lives through positive thoughts and actions and in so doing be at one with the universe.

You can write your own prayers and memorize them if you wish or vary them from day to day depending on where you would like your focus to be.

Types of Meditation

Of course, there are other types of meditation.

Probably the most well-known is Transcendental Meditation (TM) made famous by Maharishi Mahesh Yogi. He taught it first in India and went on several world tours in the early sixties. It became popular when the Beatles and the Beach Boys adopted this practice. Transcendental Meditation involves the silent repetition of a mantra, (usually a Sanskrit word or sound) for 15 - 20 minutes per day.

Transcendental Meditation is led by a certified TM trainer who gives the mantra. It is taught through a prescribed program, which for years was done in person but now is taught on-line. TM is beneficial in promoting relaxation, lowering blood pressure, and reducing stress just as other meditation techniques.

Because TM requires a greater level of commitment to learn and develop the practice, here are four other types of meditation that you might find more accessible:

1. Mindfulness

The simplest of meditations. It is a method of focusing on normal breathing. As you do this, thoughts will enter your mind. You notice them but do not judge them and let them pass. You then return to your breath. This happens repeatedly until you notice you have fewer thoughts. This practice combines awareness with concentration, making it an excellent practice in preparing for deeper types of meditation.

If you want to try mindfulness, set a timer for 10 or 15 minutes. This will allow you to focus on the meditation to see how long you can hold your concentration. As you begin to master your thoughts, you can combine mindfulness with other techniques, such as candle gazing.

Light a candle, and stare at the flame. Whenever your mind wanders, come back to focusing on the flame. This can be done with an actual candle or with an app. Another technique is to silently repeat a word, such as peace or love. When your mind wanders, just refocus on your selected word.

As we wake in the morning, we are in-between a state of sleeping and wakefulness. Hypnopompia is the scientific word for this transitional state versus the term hypnagogia, which is the period between being awake and falling asleep. Both have similar manifestations.

This in-between time is brief, but meaningful. It is a time when reality warps and we experience sensations, visions, and sounds that do not seem to have any meaning with our outer consciousness.

We can be more aware of this time as we awaken and use it to set an intention for the day, which may have an impact beyond our normal beta brain wave state during waking hours. During this transitional phase, we are in the theta brain wave state often attained in meditation. In this very relaxed state, we can imagine the day going smoothly with joy and fulfillment.

As you become aware you are waking up, you can put on headphones and listen to binaural beats, which can prolong the period you are in the theta state. There are various options on YouTube as well as gamma wave beats, the highest brain wave frequency, which can improve focus and memory. This can be a nice transition from sleeping to getting ready for daily activities. Just doing 5 to 10 minutes of listening to these beats can enhance overall well-being. This may be a nice transition if you have trouble getting out of bed.

2. Guided Meditation

This is meditation led by a teacher, either in person or by audio or video. If you are new to meditation, this might be a good way to begin.

It can be beneficial to have someone else plan the meditation, so you do not have to focus your attention on this aspect of the process. With today's technology, guided meditations are widely available on YouTube, audio platforms like Spotify and the websites of spiritual healers and teachers.

In a guided meditation, instructions are given that tell you when to open and close your eyes and when to breathe deeply or hold your breath. You might go on a guided journey that involves visualization. There are also meditation videos with just instrumental sound where you can watch some of the very calming videos with beautiful images. Even experienced mediators use guided meditation apps as part of their toolkit due to the easy availability of high-quality content.

Once you determine what benefits you would like out of your meditation practice, you can begin to peruse what's available, including many apps for meditation practices, such as Headspace, Calm® and The Mindfulness.

3. Japa Meditation

This is a practice which comes from traditions of Hinduism and Buddhism. It involves the repetition of a mantra using prayer beads. The word *"japa"* comes from a Sanskrit word meaning *"murmur"*.

This type of meditation is often done by speaking out loud, but usually in a softer voice. It can be recited silently, or you can just mouth the word. This form of meditation aims to keep your focus on a particular word or phrase as opposed to eliminating all thoughts.

The mantra aspect of the Japa Meditation is often a very sacred word, especially in the Hindu tradition. These words are sometimes various forms of God or consciousness. The word *"om"* is a common one which translates to the essence of consciousness. You can also use any word you wish depending on what resonates with you. The word *"peace"* could be used as a calming term.

The role of the prayer beads, called Mala Beads, is the main practice of Japa Meditation. The name *"mala"* from Sanskrit means *"garland"* - representative of a string of beads. The beads are used as counting aides, guiding when to switch to the next bead based on the mantra repetition.

The traditional mala has 108 beads, which corresponds to the number of letters in the Sanskrit alphabet. The teacher or guru bead is bigger or a different color and acts as the starting and ending point. Malas are made from various materials such as wood, organic seeds or crystal gemstones.

To use the mala beads, begin at one side of the largest bead. Use your thumb or middle finger and work your way around the mala heading clockwise. Once you have made your way around the mala, flip it around without touching the teacher bead, and work your way back, touching each bead as you say the mantra. You can do this as many times as you wish.

A japa ring can also be used. It is a specially designed ring with bumps worn on one of the fingers. The ring is turned with the thumb, each turn making one repetition of the mantra.

4. Progressive Muscle Relaxation/Body Scan

This type of meditation was created back in the 1920's by an American physician, Edmund Jacobson. It is based on the premise that physical relaxation leads to mental relaxation. This is a good form of meditation if you have trouble calming yourself down. If you sit or lie down to meditate, you may feel restless, or parts of your body may feel tense. If so, try this meditation. Start with a scan of your body. If your leg feels restless, just shake it out or stand up and walk around and then sit back down. Do this with any part of your body that feels unsettled.

Once you feel a general sense of well-being, begin progressive relaxation. This involves tensing up parts of your body and then relaxing those parts. You can start from your head and make your way down your body or start from your toes and work your way up. Hold each muscle area tightly for about five seconds. Then exhale as you let your muscles relax for ten to twenty seconds. Once you have finished, scan your body and if any area still feels tense, repeat the process for that muscle group.

Once you feel your body is relaxed, you can return to your day or you can proceed to another form of meditation, such as listening to a guided meditation or doing a mindfulness exercise.

There are many recordings and YouTube videos available for progressive muscle relaxation techniques.

Julie's Story

Julie was very frustrated when I met her. She tried various forms of meditation for a couple of years and was unsuccessful. She had been diagnosed with an anxiety disorder and was taking medication.

She desperately wanted to get off the medication and handle her anxiety in a more natural manner. She was having unwanted side effects and when she attempted to titrate the medication down, she became very anxious. Initially, I recommended a guided meditation embedded with hypnosis techniques. Julie tried this for two weeks but could not remain quiet during the 10-minute duration. I reduced the time to five minutes. She was still unable to remain still.

Finally, I recommended Japa Meditation. She purchased a mala and had some success. She was able to go for longer periods of time without anxiety. However, her overall anxiety did not reduce. I loaned her a japa ring and encouraged her to use it whenever she felt anxious.

I instructed her to do it silently while she was in stressful meetings at work, while walking her dog or anytime she felt anxious.

It worked! It fit perfectly into her need to be moving as the movement of her thumb over the ring was very soothing to her. She measured her heart rate during this time, and it significantly decreased. Best of all, she was able to come off the anti-anxiety medication! She purchased her own beautiful ring and fully embraced this practice.

It is important to determine what benefits you would like out of your meditation practice. For example, would you like to develop a meditation practice to help you sleep better or to reduce stress and anxiety? Maybe you would like to send love and peace out into the world. Knowing what it is you want to receive from a meditation practice will help you not only choose the right technique but will most likely mean that you will choose a method that you will stay with. And that is the most important part of the process.

Now that you've got meditation options in your toolkit, it's time to delve into practice.

EXERCISE

1. Find a comfortable position, preferably wearing lose clothing. You can either sit or lie down.

2. Take three deep breaths slowly, fully breathing in and out.

3. If any area of your body feels tense, practice the progressive muscle relaxation technique for that area.

4. Begin breathing slowly at a normal rhythm, focusing on your breath.

5. Pair a phrase with your breathing, such as *"I AM Peace"*, repeating silently *"I AM"* as you inhale and *"Peace"* as you exhale.

6. Once you feel relaxed with this practice, focus your mind and enter your heart or your solar plexus and center yourself there.

7. An image may come into your mind. Perhaps a nature location or perhaps a loved one who has died. Just allow any message or experience you may have to enter your consciousness. Do this for as long as you like.

8. Once you feel complete with this image or message, focus back on your breathing.

9. Begin to think about coming back out of your meditation.

10. Move parts of your body such as wiggling your toes and, when ready, open your eyes.

11. If you like, you can record your meditation in a journal.

If you'd like to experience a recorded guided meditation, please visit **24-7flow.com.**

Chapter Four : Mind Your Mind

"Every cell in your body is eavesdropping on your thoughts."

Deepak Chopra

Do you ever find yourself in the midst of an activity when, suddenly, you become aware of the constant chatterbox that is your mind?

Most likely, unless you focus on your thoughts, you are not aware of the thousands of thoughts flowing through your mind. Like the scrolling banner on the stock market channels that constantly show the latest price changes, your mind is scrolling through thousands of thoughts, many of them repetitive, many of them negative, and many of them unconscious. And that endless chatter of the mind impacts how you feel about yourself, your body, other people, and even your ability to heal and maintain a healthy life – right down to the cellular level.

What messages do you think your mind is sending to the approximately 100 trillion cells in your body? 100 trillion cells! Wow!

When the cells are in harmony, you experience health and feel healthy. When that is not the case, then you experience dis-ease, a disharmony of the cellular landscape.

Health and healing begin at the cellular level. Groups of cells form tissues which form organs, and they are dependent upon the health of the cells within them. These cells are very small yet very important. They contain molecules and atoms which are constantly at work generating new creation. And you are always communicating with them.

If you don't mindfully communicate with your cells and give them new direction, they continue to do what they have always done and will respond to the input you've given them, almost entirely on an unconscious level. So, minding your mind is key to your overall experience of health down to each and every tiny cell. If you're wondering how you're supposed to mindfully communicate with 100 trillion cells, read on. You're about to learn some fascinating facts about the science of your amazing body.

In her book *Cell-Level Healing*, Joyce Whiteley Hawkes, PhD describes various parts of the cell:

1. The Cell Membrane helps to regulate cell activity by allowing the passage of specific materials in and out of the cell and maintains structural integrity of the cell.

2. Nanotubes transfer information between cells via biochemical packets.

3. The nucleus preserves the codes of life (DNA-chromosomes).

4. The Endoplasmic Reticulum is responsible for the final production of structural and enzymatic proteins.

5. Mitochondria produce all the energy the cells need.

Right now, you're probably having brain-freeze remembering all those high-school biology classes you skipped out on. Not to worry. Today you can see videos on YouTube that show what the insides of your cells look like. It's as if within every single cell is a universe, and when that universe is healthy, you feel at your best.

You most likely won't have the opportunity to look at a cell under an electron microscope, but the advancement of science enables you to get a very good idea about the wondrous activity that occurs within and between them. Viewing pictures that have been greatly enlarged by a million times and watching videos of cells in action can give you a whole new appreciation of these elements within your body.

If you're thinking I'm someone who was always a science nerd, you'd be wrong. In fact, I wasn't interested in science, and I was even less interested in biology. All I remember from high school was dissecting a frog and when the teacher wanted us to cut into a cat, I totally lost interest, thinking with apprehension about my tabby at home. In college I avoided all courses having to do with anatomy as some of my friends had to memorize hundreds of muscle types and other parts and systems of the body.

However, when I had the opportunity one time to view blood under a microscope I was blown away. I had no idea how complex and intricate blood was when viewed up close and personal.

I remember thinking it looked like a painting that could be hanging in a museum in the modern art section. That experience made me realize

I had absolutely no sense of what was happening within my own body. I knew about the major systems and organs and loosely what their function was, but I wasn't truly aware of anything except perhaps the surface of my skin.

Years later I still have only scratched the surface, so to speak, of how my body functions daily, but I do have a much greater appreciation for everything it does for me.

Your cells regenerate every 28 days. Your cells have memory and if you don't give them something new to do, they will keep repeating the same old thing repeatedly. You need to give them new direction. Those distorted thoughts and feelings you have can cause disharmony in the cells, and disharmony equals dis-ease.

Did you know that when you are afraid, that fear goes into your cells which causes them to contract? By minding your mind, you can directly communicate with your cells and let them know they don't need to suffer anymore. You can treat them with the respect they deserve for their constant dedication and unending effort to do the work they were designed to do.

You have within you an energy source that constantly creates. In fact, you are energy and have energy fields around you that are always in communication. When minor things happen, such as a cut on your leg, your body springs into action, repairing the area and returning it to its normal state. When major things occur, such as cancer, when cells begin to duplicate more than they should, your body still retains the information to get back to health. Here is a quick exercise for you to do to mindfully work on cellular healing:

1. Watch a video of healthy cells and have pictures so you can visualize them with your eyes closed.

2. Move into a meditative state by sitting or lying down. Take a few deep breaths and use whichever method you prefer to relax your body.

3. Visualize an area of your body you would like to heal and surround the cells with love and light. See them luminous and shining brightly.

4. Activate these cells by sending energy into them and reassuring them all is well and give them direction with your mind to do their jobs in the highest manner possible.

5. Send them gratitude for all they do and for keeping you in a healthy state.

This process does not have to take long, and when you feel it's complete you can either continue to meditate or bring it to a conclusion and move on with your day. This exercise can be done at any time, but morning seems to be the best time to start the day out with a healthy mindset.

The key component of the process is frequent repetition. Regular repetition ensures that you are filled with love for your cells and totally confident in their ability to bring you into a condition of health. As you do this exercise you step into flow, and you can experience that ease of flow within the boundaries of each and every day.

Sophia's Story

Sophia found herself in the emergency room with severe tick bites on her belly. She was diagnosed with Lyme disease. She suffered terribly for months with extensive treatment for her symptoms. She was unable to fully participate in her life, limited in what she could do, unable to plan for any events ahead of time. It took her many months to fully recover.

Almost a year to the date of her Lyme disease diagnosis, she was bitten again and had two tick bites. She decided right then and there that she could not go through what she had just endured the previous year. She took some deep breaths and calmed herself. Visualizing the area around the tick bites, Sophia expressed gratitude to the cells responsible for maintaining health in that area. She thanked them for handling this tick invasion on her behalf. She surrounded the area with light and surrendered with love, knowing the cells would do their work and not allow a reaction to set in.

Sophia did not go to the emergency room until she was confident her body had healed itself. When she did go and get tested for Lyme disease, she tested negative. That was several years ago and to this day, she has not been afflicted with this disease again, even though she has been bitten many times.

Mind Your Mind with Gratitude

I challenge you to look at the cellular activity in your body and develop a greater level of gratitude for your body.

It can be difficult to view your body in a positive way in today's world. You are constantly bombarded with products to improve the way you look and medicines to treat illnesses, even some illnesses that don't exist!

However, the first rule to heal your body is to develop an appreciation for the miracle of life and an awe for how well your body functions. Most of what your body does is behind the scenes and occurs automatically without your conscious awareness. Which means you don't think about your body's inner workings, until something malfunctions and then you react.

Changing how you view yourself allows you to be proactive and keep your body healthy in mind, body and spirit. Once you have a clear flow of life energy you can deal more easily with anything that may happen to your body including injuries and illnesses. You can also counteract the usual problems that arise with aging.

Here's the secret sauce – it's gratitude.

Begin with a practice of gratitude. Viewing life with a glass half full versus a glass half empty attitude has many benefits.

The positive results are well-known and available to everyone:

- Stronger immunity

- Lowered blood pressure

- Better sleep

- Higher levels of positive emotions

- Forgiving more easily

- Feeling less lonely and isolated

- Wanting to be more helpful, generous and compassionate

- Improved self-esteem

Minding your Mind with gratitude is not only easy but it can help you connect with the child you once were who had an optimistic outlook on life and dreams of what was possible.

Next time you are in a bookstore or gift shop, pick up a Gratitude Journal. Find something beautiful that speaks to your sensibility and use the journal to jot down daily what you are grateful for that day.

Writing in a journal has the magical aspect of taking what is in the energy of the mind and making it concrete and tangible with the hand. It's an old method often taught to students on the benefits of taking notes with memory. The same technique is still effective.

Decorate your journal – really make it an art project with words and images that bring you joy. Connect with the child within and have a goal of writing down five things daily, regardless of the circumstances of the day. As you continue this practice, it will get easier to find the five things and perhaps harder to stop at just five!

Gratitude can easily become a way of life.

If a journal doesn't appeal, make yourself a Gratitude Jar. Find a jar or box that you love and decorate it however you like. Put some paint, stickers, ribbons and glitter on it. It's yours to create in whatever way appeals to you. Daily write little notes of gratitude. It may be a word, the name of a person, a beloved pet, the beauty of the sky – you get the idea.

Fill the gratitude jar daily to overflowing and watch your energy and your mood lift higher and higher. If you're feeling a little down one day, go to the jar and pull one of the messages. When the jar is full, if you are artistically minded you can create a collage of all the messages, images and colored papers you put in the jar and begin again.

Now that you have some options for putting gratitude practice into your life, let's get back to the body.

Gratitude leads to an appreciation of the body that flows from the heart and encompasses the entire body. Be grateful to YOURSELF.

This is how grace enters your body. When you judge yourself in a negative manner you close off from the natural flow which results in energy blockages and eventually illnesses.

Body appreciation is an important step in keeping yourself healthy and keeping a positive mental health attitude. If you begin to love the internal aspects of what your body does for you, you can extend this love to how you look and not be so self-critical of your body image and personality.

This can lead to a change in perspective regarding how you live your life. Instead of battling against your body, fighting disease and aging, you can be proactive and begin to love what you've been given as a vehicle to get you through this lifetime. Once you develop awareness of the miraculous nature of how your body functions, you can move from the biological attributes to a feeling of sacredness and awe. From this state you can use your thoughts and feelings to move from disease to health and then to optimal wellness. You'll step into 24/7 flow.

There is an esoteric teaching which says we have a quantum body or *"smart body".* This is a frequency within our own field that we can access to help us heal. It is apparently assigned to us such as the concept of a guardian angel in Catholicism.

Whether we embrace this idea or not, we can use it to accent our healing techniques. Our smart body holds all the information we need to direct our cells to realign themselves when they are out of order and creating unhealthy conditions in our bodies.

I like to use this to help me remember to stay in a lighter mood while I'm doing the healing techniques so as not to lower my frequency. I have given a name to my smart body, and I think of her as a very smart friend that knows my body better than I do.

I don't want to lose the burning desire I have to heal, nor do I want to slip into desperation. I move into a state of great love for my body/cells and create an adoration for the light coming through. Then I enjoy creating various healing images, playing with them and relishing this practice. It turns into a feeling of exhilaration.

EXERCISE

If you are feeling overwhelmed by this new understanding of how miraculous your body and mind are, then perhaps your smart body can help.

Take a few moments to sit comfortably and relax using your breath to quiet the mind and allow the body to soften. In your mind, give thanks to your smart body and ask your smart body what name it would like to be known as.

Allow yourself to go with the first name that pops in. Don't judge. Accept. Visualize your smart body as the optimally healthy version of yourself. Allow that vision of yourself at optimal health to inspire you. Let it be a road map for a journey that your smart body will take you on.

Trust the communication you have with your smart body. Connect with it daily and allow that relationship to become stronger. As you do so, follow your intuition as to healthy changes you can make that move you along the path of optimal health.

Keep a journal of your daily interactions with your smart body for at least one month, always expressing gratitude for the connection. At the end of the month notice how you feel mentally and physically.

Work with the visualizations and the five-step process to work with your cells. What you will notice is that your love for your physical body will expand as your intimacy with the wonder of your own creation opens your heart.

Just like Sophia's ability to heal her Lyme Disease, you have the power to shift your perspective and become an active conscious partner in creating your best and healthiest life.

Chapter Five : Your Vagus Nerve

"Emotional regulation is arguably the most valuable skill a person can acquire in their lifetime."

Paul Canali, MD

In 2011, after completing my year of shamanic energy medicine studies, I visited my son in New York City, where he was living and working fresh out of college. At dinner he shared that he thought I seemed different. *"You are more able to pay attention to me,"* he said, fighting back tears.

So much of his childhood and adolescent years were captured in that one sentence. With his sister's death, the whole world felt terribly cruel and unsafe – for the both of us. We lived with our bodies in fight-flight-freeze for so many years – distracted, and easily triggered, defensive, or totally shut down. I so wish I had known then about the Vagus Nerve.

The vagus nerve is your body's superhighway – it goes from your brain stem all the way down to your stomach, wrapping around all your organs on its way. It is the sender and receiver of information, controlling things like your digestion, heart rate, voice, mood, and immune system. Importantly, when you take good care of this nerve, you have more empathy, compassion, mental clarity, social connection, and emotional stability in your life.

Unbeknownst to me, my year-long shamanic studies were toning my vagus nerve, resetting my autonomic nervous system, as I later learned from a colleague and mentor Paul Canali, MD, the founder of Unified Therapy and an expert on the body's vagus nerve. Spending extended time in nature, sound healing ceremonies with drums, rattles and chanting, cold water swims, and fire breath breathing exercises moved me out of the fight-flight-freeze response into a calm, *"digest and rest"* state. With this shift came my ability to be more present with my son – and myself.

The self-regulating practices that were part of my program have modern-day versions that you are learning about in this book. These practices are crucial for staying in a positive state of mind, to be in flow. They help you train your mind, which is the core of happiness. The renowned scientist Albert Einstein stated that *"The most important decision we make is whether we believe we live in a friendly or hostile universe. The answer we find determines what we do with our entire lives."* If we decide the universe is friendly, we spend our time building bridges. Otherwise, we spend our time building walls, using our resources to destroy all that is unfriendly.

With continual use, the practices you are learning here will gradually shift your perspective towards a positive outlook, hopefully settling your mind on the idea that the world is a friendly place.

It's time to learn more about the vagus nerve. To perceive the world as friendly, in today's chaos, requires the conscious effort to reset your autonomic nervous system – you do this by activating your vagus nerve, using simple techniques that are easily built into your daily life. To take care of your vagus nerve means that you keep it toned or activated. The techniques presented here help you do just that. You don't have to be a scientist to understand what the vagus nerve controls, but it helps to have some information so you can visualize your vagus nerve helping you maintain a healthy nervous system, and a mind at peace and in balance.

The vagus nerve is an important part of your body's autonomic nervous system (ANS). The ANS functions to maintain and balance your life. It has three branches or parts.

The Enteric Brain or Gut Brain

Imagine your gut having its own brain - it's surprising, right? Well, here's another surprising fact: the health of your gut is connected to your mood. Studies have linked depression to poor gut health. So, the better your gut health, the happier and more motivated you feel.

Why? This is actually because the lining of your gut produces many neurotransmitters - chemical messengers. In fact, it makes 90% to 95% of the body's serotonin, a neurotransmitter that helps you feel happy, get enough sleep, and have a good appetite. There's also dopamine, another neurotransmitter in your gut, that keeps you motivated, and GABA, which works to calm the brain. When your gut is healthy, it effortlessly produces these chemicals, and through the vagus nerve, it connects them to the higher brain, contributing to your overall well-being.

The Parasympathetic System

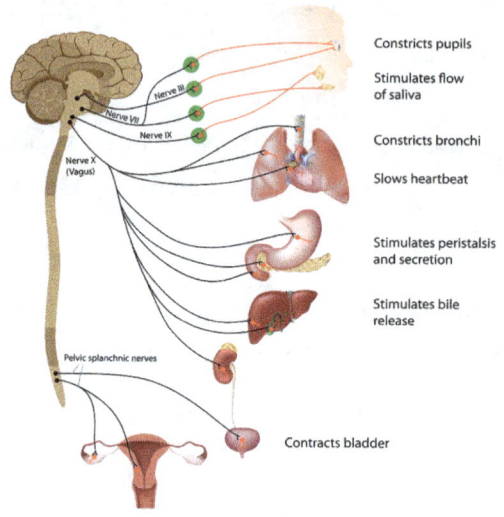

The parasympathetic branch (via the vagus nerve) is more in control when you are healing, resting, sleeping, digesting, after exercise, and in meditation or other relaxation practices.

The Sympathetic System

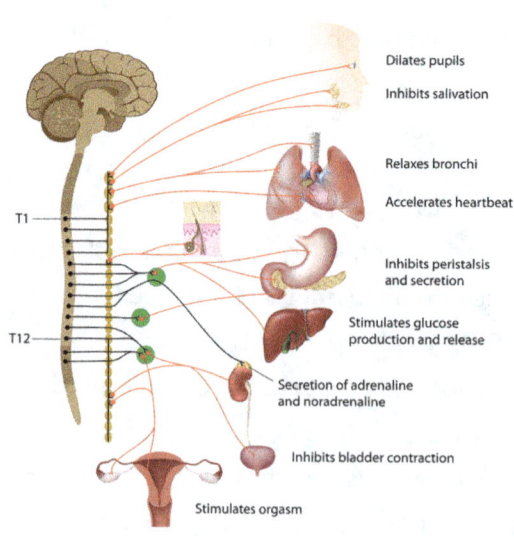

The sympathetic branch is more in control when stressed, injured, fearful, exercising or in "Fight or Flight" mode.

These two branches work together in opposing each other to keep the body in balance. If either branch is persistently more elevated, it is not healthy. This would result in an imbalance in your ANS. Research has shown that significant imbalances in your ANS can result in problems anywhere in your body. This includes head and neck pain, chronic fatigue, gastritis, irritable bowel syndrome and even auto-immune diseases.

Until recently, little was known about the vagus nerve's importance in preventing and lessening the impact of stress. Now that many studies have linked a healthy vagus nerve with low levels of cortisol, less overall stress and with the ability to cope with stressful situations, it's being widely referred to as the secret weapon against stress.

Cat's Story

My recent exploration into stressors and stress responses was sparked while teaching my vagus nerve course to Cat, a mother of three.

She shared that her current stress levels are much lower than when her first child was young and diagnosed with autism. Now, as a mother of three, she faces additional stressors with two more children also diagnosed on the autism spectrum, and her husband being on the spectrum as well.

Cat clarified that despite the increased stressors, she feels more in control of her life and better equipped to handle her responsibilities as a mother, especially compared to her early days as a new mother lacking the skills and knowledge needed to support her daughter.

Cat has more stressors, yet she experiences less stress. Cat went on to share that lowering expectations also reduced her stress which gave her more ability to listen to her own inner guidance system. Although she came to me to learn how to create more flow in her life, she had already overcome so much.

This can be you. Your stressors can ebb and flow, with you remaining balanced and calm. You can achieve balance and flow, like Cat, by gaining more knowledge and skills and by toning your vagus nerve. This will result in greater emotional resiliency – the highest form of personal empowerment.

The time to do this is now. It is time to develop your emotional fortitude. Due to the high levels of chaos and global disorder, becoming engulfed in the sadness, grief and fears of others is a real possibility.

In today's world, stress triggers and/or perceived threats are so prevalent that a vast majority of people are living emotionally unregulated and stressed. The once infrequent lion attack has been replaced with a continuance of potential dangers from natural disasters, ecological losses, pandemics, school violence, mass shootings, looming or actual financial losses, among others.

These threats can seep into your subconscious mind. While the subconscious mind can differentiate between real and perceived threats, the constant bombardment of threats causes the fear center, the amygdala, to expand. This results in heightened fear responses, leading to decreased cognitive function and creativity. Toning your vagus nerve can help counteract these effects and restore balance to your life. In such a state, flow is not an option; fluid thinking, and creativity suffer. So, let's get you toning your vagus nerve!

Toning the Vagus Nerve

Toning the vagus nerve involves engaging in specific lifestyle habits aimed at enhancing its function. Research indicates that improving vagal tone is associated with several outcomes, including:

TONING EFFECTS
Lowers Heart Rate
Lowers Blood Pressure
Reduces Stress Hormones (Cortisol, Adrenaline and Norepinephrine)
Improves Output of Melatonin (Sleep)
Improves Output of Oxytocin (Trust)
Increases Lymphatic Circulation (Protects Against Infections and Removes Waste)
Enhances Release of Endorphins (Feel Good)
Promoting the Production of Stomach Acid and Digestive Enzymes
Increases Release of Serotonin and Dopamine
Increases Heart Rate Variability

EFFECTS ON HEALTH AND WELLBEING
Less Stress and Burnout
Improved Mental Health
Improved Heart Health
Improved Digestion
Easier Mood Regulation
Reduced Inflammation
Strengthened Immune System

There are numerous ways to tone your vagus nerve. The most accessible one available to you at any moment during the day is working with your breath.

Conscious Breathing

You are asking me to become aware of my breathing? Did I get that right? Yes, that is exactly what conscious breathing is – being aware of every breath. All the while, being aware of nothing else. Giving your busy mind a rest as your deep breaths go about activating your vagus nerve, reducing your heart rate, letting your mind and body know that for the moment all is good.

By the law of averages, you will take 670 million breaths in your lifetime. As you already know, you will take most of these breaths without thinking of them. In the modern world, the important thing is to get air into our lungs, which is done automatically thanks to the good work of our brain stem. To breathe we do not need to give it much thought and we don't.

However, this has not always been the case. Ancient scholars and mystics understood the importance of breathwork and believed that to live a long healthy, full, and joyful life, one needed to understand the importance of the breath. They knew what science has confirmed – that we exist in a quantum field of potent energy. When we bring this energy into our bodies intentionally and deeply, through extended breathing, there are significant health benefits.

In ancient China around 400 BCE, the Chinese Tao, the texts that were written to describe *the way of the universe and how to best live* dedicated seven books about how to breathe.

One method they taught was taking deep breaths into your belly to move your energy, called qi, around your body. Nowadays, you might see this technique in yoga classes.

For Judeo-Christians, we kept it short and to the point. In both the New and Old Testaments, breath is equated with God's Spirit, as it is for the Hindus. The Buddhists use breathing to extend life and to reach higher planes of consciousness. The yogic practice of focusing on breath is called pranayama of which there are a dizzying number of ways to work with one's breath – all in service to maintaining good physical, mental, and emotional and spiritual well-being.

Hence, it's not unexpected to discover that one of the most assured ways to stay in flow is by incorporating slow, deep, rhythmic breaths into your routine. As you learn and practice each of the five simple breathing techniques explained here, find one you are most comfortable with and make that one your practice. It is up to you which one.

Before we jump into exploring the five simple and invigorating breathing techniques, I want to underscore a crucial health factor. You have a nose for a good reason, and you need to use it. The mental and physical health conditions associated with mouth breathing include gum disease, bad breath, risk of more cavities, restless sleep patterns, and recurrent throat infections. Importantly, children with breathing problems such as snoring, mouth breathing, or apnea are 40–100 times more likely to develop behavioral problems resembling ADHD.

I visualize our ancient ancestors standing with their hands on their hips, saying, *"We told you so."* Lawyer and ethnographer George Catlin, traveled and lived among 50 Native American tribes in North and South America. His book, *The Breath of Life*, documented his travels and what he learned.

Everywhere he went he observed the practice of mothers calmly closing their infant's mouth after each feeding and pinching it closed if they noticed it open at other times of the day. Upon inquiry, he learned that breathing through the mouth was believed to sap the body of strength, deform the face and cause stress and disease.

Caitlin had once been a mouth breather himself – adhering to the principle of *"like attracts like"* as he roamed the West, he found himself among the Native Americans. Caitlin grappled with snoring and had a range of respiratory issues, including spitting up blood during childhood and adolescence. Remarkably, upon successfully retraining himself to breathe through his nose, all his health troubles vanished.

If you are a mouth breather, you are in the majority, but the solution is easy. Simply apply a small piece of tape to close your mouth during sleeping hours. Use the tape throughout the day as much as is necessary. The tape can be small, postage stamp size and over the center of the lips. 3M Nexcare Durapore (durable cloth) tape is the most popular suggestion.

Mouth breathing may be a symptom of other health-related conditions, such as enlarged adenoids, nasal congestion, or a deviated septum. As such, anyone that frequently breathes through their mouth should seek advice from their doctor.

Breathing and the Vagus Nerve

Recently, the effectiveness of breathwork has become an interest to researchers. So much so that, in a 2018 systematic internet search of medical databases, using words related to the benefits of breathing techniques, 2,461 research studies were identified. The studies showed that taking time each day – 10 to 20 minutes or longer – to tone the vagus nerve by breathing deeply has significant health benefits.

Five Breath Practices

As you have learned there are many different breathwork practices to choose from. Again, we apply the rule, choose the one you will do. All forms of deep breathing when practiced daily for 10 to 20 minutes at a time are associated with important health benefits:

- Decreased stress

- Increased calm

- Pain relief

- Stimulation of the lymphatic system (Detoxifies the body)

- Improved immunity

- Increased energy

- Lowered blood pressure

- improved digestion

- Better posture

- Increased heart rate variability

- Increased clarity of thought

- Increased oxygen to the brain

- Improved focus and ability to learn

Practice 1 : The Physiological Sigh

Physiological Sigh is a pattern of breathing that rapidly reduces the stress load on the body and can be done at any time or place. It was discovered in the 1930's and recently rediscovered by Professor Dr. Jack Feldman, a neurobiologist at UCLA.

The technique is simple. It is a double inhale followed by an extended exhale. The first inhale is long and the second is short. Two or three of the Physiological Sighs immediately slow down the heart which activates the vagus nerve and turns on the body's parasympathetic system.

Practice 2 : Soft Belly Breathing

This is one of the simplest breathing patterns to use and an easy one to start with.

- Find a comfortable place to sit. Sit up straight with shoulders relaxed, and your feet on the floor.

- Place your hands on your belly and allow your abdomen to relax.

- Soften your focus or close your eyes if you are comfortable doing so.

- Breathe deeply through your nose. Notice the expansion of your lower abdomen, ribs, upper chest, and throat.

- Exhale slowly through your nose. Notice the complete release of air from your lower abdomen.

Follow the rhythm of your breath. Set a timer to continue for 10 minutes. When your mind wanders, gently return your thoughts back to your breath. Sit quietly and notice how you are feeling. See if you notice a slight change in perception. Your brain waves may have slowed down along with your heart rate. You may feel slightly dizzy.

Practice 3 : The Resonant (Coherent) 5.5 Breath

This breathwork technique is my favorite. Before Ubiquity University's pilgrimage to Chartres, France in 2022, the university president started his morning podcast with this breathwork.

I joined in with hundreds of others worldwide, breathing in and out for 5.5 minutes. James Nestor, an expert on breath, calls it the perfect breath because it puts the heart, lungs, and circulation into a harmonized state, where the body works at its best.

To try this breath: For 5.5 minutes, inhale for about 5.5 seconds, then exhale for 5.5 seconds. Your breathing should feel effortless and circular, with a small pause between inhale and exhale. Interestingly, when you breathe this way, you take in about 5.5 liters of air each minute. Some apps, like Paced Breathing and My Cardiac Coherence, have timers and visual guides. James Nestor's website has information about the 5.5 Breath, and other instructional videos by Harvard doctors, yogis, and practitioners worldwide.

Practice 4 : The 4-4-4-4 Box Breath

Feeling tense – try the Box Breath. Navy SEALs use the Box Breath technique to stay calm and focused in tense situations. It's simple.

- Inhale to a count of 4
- Hold 4
- Exhale 4
- Hold 4
- Repeat

Try at least six rounds, more if necessary to fully relax.

Practice 5 : The 2 to 1 Breath

This breathing pattern requires exhaling for twice the time you inhale. Longer exhales than inhales make for a stronger 'rest and digest' response. For this breath you follow the same steps as with soft belly breathing. You can begin with an inhale to the count of 3 and a slow exhale to the count of 6. Repeat.

During your exhale, gently pull in your abdominal muscles to gently push out additional air. This helps release waste gases such as carbon dioxide more completely. Try to complete 10 rounds. 4 inhales to 8 exhales works also.

Breathwork and Healing Light

In an earlier chapter, you learned how to bring healing to the cells in your body. You learned to visualize the area of the body you would like to heal and with your mind, surround those cells with love and light. In this chapter, you learned about five breathing techniques, known to help you bring balance and calm to your mind and body.

EXERCISE

Bring the visualization technique into your breathing exercises.

Take the 4-4-4-4 Box Breath, for example. Inhale to the count of 4, imagining the breath as a conduit for love and light. Picture this positive energy entering through the crown of your head, a concept rooted in yoga traditions, and traveling deep into your abdomen.

On your exhale, visualize the outbreath carrying away anything not in harmony with your highest well-being. It may be sadness, worry, guilt, or fear – there's no need to label what needs to be released. Simply trust your body's innate wisdom to know and release what is necessary.

Chapter Six :
Music and Sound as Medicine

*"Music is a moral law. It gives soul to the universe,
wings to the mind, flight to the imagination, and charm
and gaiety to life and to everything."*

Plato

Music plays a unique role in your life. It helps you move, dance, sing, feel joy, reminisce, and even gives you a sense of self.

The connection of sound and music to health and wellness is being explored around the world. For example, just by listening to the music you like, you are boosting the connectivity in your brain related to empathy. While you are listening to your favorite songs, you are boosting the connectivity in your memory centers and social-emotional centers. Music has other effects, many of them related to the key public health issues we are facing today, i.e., memory, mood, and movement. That is because listening to music is a full brain workout.

You have undoubtedly had the sensation of music vibrating through you, unexpectedly altering your mood. Maybe it evoked a sudden smile, feelings of joy, or an urge to dance. Or perhaps feelings of melancholy, sadness, or a foreboding. Music's ability to evoke emotion is most transparent when watching a movie, the subtle nuances of sound effects seamlessly enhancing your emotional responses, adding depth to your movie experience. But what about the power of music and sound to heal? Have you had that experience? Do you think it is possible?

Twelve years ago, I would have found the question odd. However, that was prior to encountering two remarkable individuals; destiny intertwined our paths, compelling us to collaborate in new approaches to health and wellness.

It was September 2011, I found myself standing outside an architecturally exquisite Spanish-style mega mansion in one of the most exclusive residential areas of Miami. It was a fundraising event. Notably, a newfound friend's family foundation was partially sponsoring the beginnings of an alternative medicine program for the University of Miami's School of Medicine. Considering the institution was both my alma mater and my professional place of employment for 12 years, I was enthused about new approaches to healthcare being introduced. My resignation a few years earlier was motivated by the strong feeling that there was a better way to deliver health care.

While waiting in line to enter the event, I turned to the gentleman standing next to me. His name was Dr. Eugene Ahn and he explained that he was an oncologist, specializing in breast cancer. Within minutes we were joking – keenly observing the notable contrast between our apparent income and that of the wealthy donors there to support the foundation. A few days prior he had been engaged in conversation with the renowned integrative medicine doctor, Andrew Weil. When asked, *"What is the most important service an oncologist can provide to his patients?"* Dr. Weil responded, *"Arts in medicine."*

Remarkably, I had just returned from a summer intensive program at the University of Florida's medical school, witnessing how they include music, dance, painting, and ceramics in their hospitals and clinics. I learned for example, having a window in your hospital room means your stay could be 2 to 3 days less than without a window. Nature scenes hung on the walls had similar impact. And music slows down one's heart rate, calming the body which allows it to heal faster. I left motivated to champion this budding form of medicine.

There we stood: two souls fated to unexpectedly meet in this improbable location. Our conversations about bringing the healing arts to the University of Miami's medical school began that evening and continued the next day and the next. In one of our conversations, Eugene suggested I speak with Loren Oliveira, co-founder of an award-winning female vocalist non-profit organization, the Brazilian Voices. She, along with other members, had sung at the bedside of one of Eugene's cancer patients. His patient remained eternally grateful, and Eugene was inspired.

Our early meetings with the Brazilian Voices resulted in a small contract with the university's cancer center and Eugene and I joined their board of directors. In 2023, Brazilian Voices performed in fifteen different healthcare facilities, including children's ICUs, delivering 147 arts and healing performances, and leaving a positive imprint on over

22,000 individuals. The success of Brazilian Voices mirrors the growing recognition of the profound impact that sound and music can have on our well-being.

Today, there is broad recognition and therapeutic potential of sound and music, both for personal use and in clinical and hospital settings. And you can reap the full benefit of this evolving landscape.

What You Need to Know

You don't have to be a scientist or musicologist to use the powerful healing potential of sound. But you do need to understand some basics so the choices you make reflect your goals of living in flow. When people talk about the impact of music on their mood it's often because music can make them feel better almost instantaneously. Have you ever wondered why?

Think of a piece of music or a favorite song or melody that, when you hear it, puts you in a good mood. As that song or piece of music plays, the sound waves hit your ears, and are converted to nerve impulses that travel not to just one area of the brain but several, including the area that releases dopamine. Dopamine is a chemical that brings pleasure and motivation.

Another reason is that music carries emotional content, and the melodies and lyrics can resonate with your own emotions. When you connect with the music your mood begins to match the emotions in the music. Slow-tempos and calming music can lower your cortisol level (a stress hormone) and help you relax. Feelings of worry and anxiety can melt away, improving your overall mood.

If you answered the self-assessment in the first chapter as someone who experiences anxiety, then music is one of the tools to put in your toolkit. It's one of the tools to help you ease into 24/7 flow.

There are as many ways to heal with music and sound as there are individuals. Have you heard of something called the Monochord Bed? If not, then prepare to be inspired by how a simple device can offer healing in a new way.

Paula's Story

In 2016 I went through a dark period in my life. I felt depressed, loss of direction and low motivation. I consulted a long-time colleague, Vanessa Cisneros, and went for a sound therapy consult. I loved laying on her Monochord bed, which looked like an oversized massage table, as she stroked the seventy strings that were attached to its underside. Within just a few minutes, I could feel a vibration throughout my body, my mind stopped ruminating and I began to relax. By hour's end an overall sense of peace had washed over me.

After, I asked her about the Monochord. She explained that the strings are tuned to a single note (in her case, C) which allows sound to resonate within the body. The sound naturally targets areas where the energy flow is obstructed; its ability to entrain the brain facilitates the release of subconscious burdens, making space for new growth and clarity.

In discussing further, she explained that her patients have a wide range of experiences. From a deep connection with themselves and their surroundings, often leading to profound insights and healing. To seeing vivid imagery, encountering past loved ones, or feeling a heightened connection to the universe. They also frequently describe feelings of peace, joy, and increased vitality following sessions.

That was my experience. She shared that she felt it a privilege to accompany individuals on their healing journeys and to witness their restoration of balance and harmony. I left reminding myself, there are so many interesting ways to heal.

Your Amazing Brain!

The role of music on the brain has to do with your limbic system, a group of interconnected structures of the brain referred to as the emotional center. Here are four of the centers and how they interact with music.

1. **Amygdala:** The amygdala is your fear evaluation center. As it relates to music, it helps determine whether the music is perceived as happy, sad, exciting, or calming. And that helps you process those emotions.

2. **Hippocampus:** The hippocampus is one of your primary memory centers. As you hear music it is involved in encoding these musical memories and connects the emotional content with the where-what-and-when contextual information. It contributes to why listening to music while learning new information can be helpful.

3. **Nucleus accumbens:** Music has a special power to lift your mood due to the nucleus accumbens. When you listen to music that you really enjoy and resonate with emotionally, the nucleus accumbens gets into action. It releases dopamine, which helps you feel happy and motivated.

4. **Hypothalamus:** When you listen to slow and calming music, the hypothalamus slows down your heart rate, eases your blood pressure, and even lowers stress hormones. It's like a musical trick that flips the chill-out switch in your body, making you feel relaxed and less stressed.

Amazing, isn't it? Of course, individual preferences play a significant role. Not all music will have the same impact on everyone. There are as many individual responses to various genres, styles, and specific songs as there are people. Your job is to figure out your specific music catalog that has you feeling calm, content, and in a good mood. An exercise at the end of this chapter will guide you into creating your personal music catalog to help you step into 24/7 flow with ease.

Music gets you moving! And movement together with music offer powerful healing opportunities. Ones I experienced for myself as I grieved the death of my daughter. For me, after my daughter's death, my strongest motivator was my son; I wanted to be there for him.

In the beginning, my steady progress came through therapy and church. My excellent listener was Helen. She was a dear friend who was faculty at the medical school in physical therapy, an exercise enthusiast. In my pondering on how to feel better, I asked, *"Knowing the research as you do, which type of exercise is the best?"* She responded, *"The one you will do."*

That year my exercise choice came wrapped in a Christmas present, from my son. A portable iPod loaded with my favorite music. My love for the outdoors and dance spontaneously blended as I listened to music while running. The slower rhythmic pace of I Love You Ya Ya Ya and the many other love songs made my hips move, arms swing, and my mind fill with warm loving thoughts.

The I love you was first directed toward my daughter and my longing to be with her again. On occasion, to a man I was dating. Years later, with my shamanic studies, I grew into the appreciation and deep love for the Earth that I have today. This love I began to feel through the embodied music – as me. A beautiful gift from son to mother – helping her heal as she helped him.

Yes, music and movement can heal grief and other deep seated emotional challenges. The degree to which it could help you depends on you tweaking the formula to perfectly match you. What do you think that formula could be? By now, you probably know that the formula is going to be one that is as unique as you are.

Whirling

"We came whirling out of nothingness, scattering stars like dust.
The stars made a circle, and in the middle, we dance."

Rumi

In 2020, a retreat announcement popped into my email in-box. It described what is known as whirling, a physically active form of meditation and a practice associated with Jalal-ad-Din Rumi, the renowned 13th century Sufi poet. Rumi's love poems always left me thirsty to understand their depth.

The idea of spinning counterclockwise to reach a calm meditative state far outweighed listening to a mindfulness meditation tape. In less than 3 minutes I registered.

Since that initial retreat, my whirling has taken me to diverse parts of the globe, joining others in a modified version of this ancient spiritual practice. Whirling requires intense concentration and a deep meditative state. Studies have shown that whirling over time can enhance mood, reduce depression, improve balance and coordination, increase flexibility and mobility, boost cardiovascular health and enhance respiratory function.

When I'm whirling, it feels like I exist between two worlds – the earthly and the spiritual. It brings me joy. If whirling appeals to you, there are excellent videos on YouTube and instructional classes that can get you started.

The Father of Music

The next time you watch Jeopardy, you might see a question that reads *Ancient Greek Philosopher Known as the Father of Music.* Press that buzzer and give a shout out to Pythagoras, philosopher, mathematician and mystic from the 6th century B.C.E., who possessed a profound understanding of the underpinnings of music. He believed the underlying structure of the cosmos, what holds the universe together, so to speak, can be understood through mathematics and the principles of geometry. He saw music as the cosmos' harmonic expression, a primal force both shaped by and for the universe.

This connection between numbers and music led to his discovery of how harmonious notes were formed; and how to apply this knowledge for tuning instruments, a method still in use today. Did you know for example that dividing a musical string in half produces a note that is an octave higher? His understanding of ratios and harmonious sounds contributed to his strong belief that the human body too was a musical instrument, with various parts of the body having their own musical note. He believed that when music was used correctly it could purify the mind, heal the soul, and restore the physical body.

Now more than two thousand years and decades of music and sound research later, scientists agree that the Father of Music was on the right track. Learning about sound frequency, brain waves, and the benefits of binaural beats will empower you with the knowledge you need to tap into the health and well-being benefits of music and sound interventions.

Understanding the term *sound frequency* gives you valuable information regarding how a particular soundtrack may affect your emotional and mental state. With this knowledge, you can make informed choices, selecting the most suitable soundtrack for your needs. Sound travels in waves and is measured in wavelengths – the distance from the crest of one wavelength to the crest of the next is considered one wavelength. Add to that, the element of speed. How fast the wave travels impacts the sound you hear. Speed is measured by how many wavelengths occur in one second, and different sounds travel at different speeds.

You may be familiar with the many APPS available now that highlight the speed factor, or the unit of measurement for the speed, called hertz (Hz). If one wavelength occurs in one second, the frequency of that wave would be 1 cycle per second or 1Hz. If there are two wavelengths in one second, the frequency would be 2Hz. You get the idea. And specific levels of Hertz can be helpful in experiencing the 24/7 flow of ease.

You may also have heard the term Binaural Beats. Binaural Beats are sound engineered by creating one soundtrack that has two slightly different frequencies. When the brain hears two frequencies at the same time, it gets confused and creates a third audible tone, which is what the brain then focuses on. This third tone is called binaural, and it is the mathematical difference between the two frequencies. For example, if the tone entering your right ear is 300Hz and the tone entering your left ear is 308Hz, then the binaural beat you will hear is 8Hz, which supports an active state of awareness.

Your Brain and Sound

What a marvelous and wondrous part of the human body and experience is the brain! That same cogitating masterwork is also the one that might have you feeling overwhelmed as it keeps track of and processes stimuli from the senses, thoughts and the autonomic functions of the body.

Modern technology provides new windows into the brain. An EEG captures the activity of the brain through sensors placed on top of the scalp. The electrical signals picked up by the sensors are recorded and the patterns that appear are used to diagnose conditions such as epilepsy, sleep apnea, and head trauma. This technology reveals there are five different kinds of brain waves. These brain waves are like a mirror into thinking and emotional states, e.g., if you are in a deep sleep, a delta brain wave is recorded. Each type of brain wave is generated from a different part of the brain and has its own frequency.

Beta Waves – Active and Alert

The brain produces beta waves when the mind is active, alert, and engaged in mental activity. Beta waves are dominant during waking hours when the mind is engaged in conscious tasks, thinking, problem-solving. They originate in the cortex, the thinking part of the brain. Beta Waves have a frequency between 13 to 30Hz. The presence of high beta brainwaves can indicate a busy and stressed mind. Your beta waves are active right now as you read this book.

Alpha Waves – Relaxed and Calm

The brain produces Alpha waves when the mind is relaxed and calm. This brain wave is prevalent when you are daydreaming, doing deep breathing exercises, or in a light relaxation. The relaxed, open focus of mindfulness increases alpha waves. It is produced by the thalamus, the brain's relay station for processing incoming and outgoing information. These waves create more of a neutral state, from which the brain can easily shift into more action or slow down. Alpha waves have a frequency between 8 and 13Hz.

Theta Waves – Deep Relaxation and Creativity

Theta waves are generated by the brain during periods of deep relaxation, hypnosis, meditation, creative visualization, and REM dreaming sleep. These waves are linked to the early stages of sleep and the waking period in the morning. Theta waves originate in the limbic brain, which governs emotion and memory. Notably, children aged from birth to 7 years predominantly experience alpha and theta brainwaves. This prevalence contributes to their active imagination, receptivity to learning, and ease with imaginative play. Theta waves have a frequency ranging between 4 and 8Hz.

Delta Waves – Deep Sleep

Delta brain waves are found most often in infants and young children and when you are in the deepest level of sleep. They are generated by the brainstem and allow the thinking brain to down-regulate and the body to rest, heal and recover. At the height of deep sleep, human growth hormones are released, repairing and strengthening the body and clearing toxins from the brain. The cycle in this frequency is between 0.5 and 4Hz.

Binaural Beats

And now we are back to sound and how to work with sound and music, empowered with the knowledge of the impact of brain waves on your experience of life. Binaural beats help to more quickly synchronize or entrain your brainwaves to match the sound frequency and its associated mental state, e.g., sleepiness, alert, creative. The following suggested uses of binaural beats are supported by research:

- **Early Evening and Bedtime:** Relaxation, Stress Reduction and Improved Sleep: Binaural beats in the lower frequency range, such as delta and theta, promote relaxation, reduce stress, and facilitate a calm and deep sleep.

- **Mid-Morning and Afternoon:** Enhanced Focus and Concentration: Higher frequency binaural beats, such as beta and gamma waves, help with concentration, alertness, and cognitive function.

- **Any Time - Mood Enhancement:** Binaural beats may be used to influence mood, with alpha and beta waves having an antidepressant or mood-boosting effects.

Hannah's Story

Hannah is a dedicated performance coach and loves to research and teach everything to do with flow. She has openly shared how her ambition was once dampened by her ADHD.

She used to struggle with focus and productivity and too easily felt off her game. Then she learned about the 'flow state' which is a state of consciousness where you feel and perform at your best. Striving to spend more time in this flow state, she did some research and discovered that binaural beats in the theta-alpha range could help. For over five years now, Hannah puts in her earbuds and listens to her binaural beats as she goes about her busy day. She shares that it has helped her access deeper levels of focus and has also significantly improved her professional and personal life.

Responses to binaural beats can vary among individuals, and more research is needed to fully understand their potential benefits and exactly how they work. Additionally, individuals with certain medical conditions or those prone to seizures should exercise caution and consult with a healthcare professional before using binaural beats.

For a direct experience of brain waves, binaural beats and your unique response, pause now and visit **24-7flow.com**. Listen to one of our sound frequencies for 3-4 minutes, preferably with headphones. Remember, it is not about whether you enjoy the sound, it is about how the sound makes you feel after listening to it.

To support your journey, we've collaborated with one of the leading authorities in sound healing, the Monroe Institute. You have direct instant access to state-of-the-art technology in the form of five unique sound frequencies, each accompanied by a comprehensive description of their therapeutic qualities.

EXERCISE

It is time for you to create a simple music catalog, one unique to you that will change and grow as you experience the impacts of different frequencies that support living a life of 24/7 flow.

You have information about brain waves, binaural beats and hopefully you've experienced some sampling from the frequencies provided above. What you might find as you develop your music catalog is that you've been attuned to many of these frequencies all along. Now you can be more purposeful in selecting music and sound that achieves the state you desire.

When I want to concentrate, I listen to (song, type of music):

_____

When I want to relax, I listen to:

_____

When I need high energy, I listen to:

_____

I never listen to: _____
as it feels uncomfortable or annoying in some way.

My favorite music to listen to is:

_____

White and Brown Noise

Do you love the sound of a vacuum cleaner, a whirring fan, the hum of an air conditioner and a strong hair dryer? Those are all examples of white noise and studies have cited improvements in mental tasks, improvements in speech recognition, writing and reading speeds. White noise has also reduced hyperactive behavior, improved attention, reduced mistakes, and helped focus on goals.

Brown Noise is a deeper and lower sound compared to other ambient noises such as white or pink noise. It's like the noise of a rumbling jet engine, heavy rainfall, or a fast-moving car. Even though there haven't been many studies, there's some evidence that listening to brown noise might help you stay focused and relaxed. To see if it works for you, try listening to brown noise soundtracks and see how you feel?

Kathy's Story

Kathy used white noise to heal an addiction. She shares, *"I have been using white noise to clear static for 12 years, day or night when my* central nervous system is overwhelmed. When I become sensitive to loud sounds or my body is tensing up around large crowds, or when I am taking in too much information at once, I put on my headphones.

"Today I am 12 years Opioid free with no medications, just self-regulation via sound therapy and other natural healing techniques. Coming off 15 years of daily use of Opioids was like having the devil's fingernails scraping my bones. It is a miracle I am alive and white noise was an important part of my healing."

The best way to develop a deeper relationship with sound and music is to experiment with a few of the techniques described here. Perhaps you can relate to the struggles or triumphs revealed in the personal stories shared. Perhaps through others' stories you can find a technique that can benefit you, a friend, colleague or family member.

If you were intrigued by one of the methods mentioned, find a way to explore it and see if it resonates with you. Music and Sound are forms of medicine, a medicine that can help you step into 24/7 flow.

Chapter Seven :
The Healing Power of Nature

"Nature itself is the best physician."

Hippocrates

Perhaps nature is already part of your life. You are an avid gardener, grow your own produce, or you love to hike, camp out, or otherwise spend time outdoors. That is wonderful, and you are already benefiting from nature's healing power.

Many Eastern cultures or Indigenous peoples have long looked to nature for healing remedies from plants and herbs that don't pose the troubling side effects that many allopathic formulations do. And Western Medicine is starting to catch up. Studies continue to show that spending time in nature helps lower stress levels, improves mood, and calms an anxious mind. And that's because you are a part of nature. Breathing fresh air and spending time in sunlight feeds body and soul.

Whatever you choose to do to incorporate nature into your daily life will be beneficial. Only you know your specific circumstances. There is no end to the creative solutions that help people bond with nature.

It doesn't matter if you are a farmer, or you are living in a studio apartment in a big city. Nature is always just outside your door. And with new approaches like living indoor plant walls, it can be inside as well. Nature is always in flow.

If you have a pet, then you know the ease of flow they demonstrate, and how much they crave being outdoors. Your connection to your pet is one of nature. As you watch their delight in exploration, play and even instinctual behaviors as predators, you are given reminders that you too are part of nature in a very real and tangible way.

But what if you could deepen your relationship with nature? Can you imagine your doctor handing you a prescription that reads, *"Cold showers seven days a week"*? Well, that is what Stanford professor and psychiatrist, Anna Lembke, does for some of her patients with addictions. More doctors are following suit. That is because their patients are feeling better, as the studies suggest. Daily cold showers and other forms of cold-water immersion are effective for depression, anxiety, mood disorders, ADHD, brain function, and stress.

If you're shivering just thinking about a cold shower, then learning how it works might be a health breakthrough for you or someone you know. It is a very straight-forward process. While the body is recovering from the shock of the chilly water - the body's 'rest and digest' system is activated, and releases the motivation neurotransmitter, dopamine, as the body strives to warm itself. Dopamine increases focus and motivation. This is particularly good news for individuals with ADHD, as this condition is associated with having a lower baseline of dopamine with difficulty to focus and stay motivated; the high sudden increase of dopamine promotes exactly what they need.

Cold water therapies have long been the province of athletics, helping peak athletes recover more quickly from injury and extend their ability to pursue their chosen careers. Golfer Gary Player, now 88 years old, moves and has the energy of a much younger man, and was known for his endurance throughout his career. His secret to living an active, long life? Eating less and taking an ice-cold bath every morning.

Wanting to lose weight? Another side benefit of cold-water immersion is fat loss. Fat loss occurs while the body is trying to regulate its temperature. Brown fat cells, responsible for the body's thermoregulation, are produced in response to the drop in body temperature. These brown fat cells increase energy burning, which heats up the body. Energy burning is the equivalent to burning calories. If you need to lose weight, you might want to slowly turn down the water temperature.

The simplest way to benefit from cold water therapy is to place a cold pack of ice on the back of your neck, where the vagal nerve clusters, for ten to fifteen minutes. This will slow down your heartbeat which in turn activates your vagus nerve, allowing your body to rest and rejuvenate.

As in the doctor's prescription, starting and/or ending your day with a cold shower is an effective way to reduce the stress load on your body. The water temperature should be around 15 degrees Celsius (60-degrees Fahrenheit). Starting your shower with warm water and slowly turning to cold makes it easier to adjust. Distracting the mind with singing and playing loud music also helps. Try to build up to 5 to 7 minutes.

If you live in colder climes, you might already be a participant in your local Polar Bear Club, starting off each new year with a plunge into a body of water near where you live. Now, armed with the health benefits, you can look for opportunities to go swimming in a lake, river, or ocean regularly.

Cold water therapy has become so popular that clinical settings and spas often have special facilities for cold water plunges. They may allow full or partial body immersion, usually into water at 15 degrees Celsius (about 60 degrees Fahrenheit). Some allow for a lying or lounging position and others only permit sitting. In general, cold-water immersions that last 10 to 15 minutes are adequate. You may need to slowly work up to that length of time.

David's Story

I met David and his partner Deborah at a spa retreat center that offered a cold-water experience in a small natural pond with a sauna close by. The pond's water temperature varies depending on the time of the year, but never rises over 60 °F. One has the option of either jumping or wading in. Either way people can only tolerate the cold water for minutes of time. After the swim, the idea is to head quickly to the nearby sauna. The contrast of cold and then heat causes a further reset of the autonomic nervous system.

When I met them, they had just been to the pond. David described the pond as super cold. Something that surprised him were the readings on his fitness device after he took the plunge. Although he felt his body took a stressful shock, his device showed exceptionally low stress. I explained to him that the cold shock activates the body's vagus nerve, triggering the *"rest and digest"* system, which immediately calms down the nervous system.

Even though David was new to the pond experience, he was no stranger to cold water showers. Describing himself as someone always seeking good health solutions, David had been inspired by Wim Hof, also known as The Iceman. He is a Dutch extreme athlete who has gained international fame for his ability to withstand extremely cold temperatures. His Wim Hof Method, a set of practices that includes cold water therapy, all aim at improving physical and mental well-being.

Inspired, David started taking cold showers as an experiment and then discovered several of the other men at work were already doing it. Working a physically demanding job with a long 2 to 4-hour drive home, he found that the cold-water showers were not only relaxing but also rejuvenating after exhausting days.

I shared that a cold shower results in a 250% increase in dopamine, providing the energy and motivation he was looking for. He said that his morning cold showers helped him wake up and start his day with an energy boost. Unsurprisingly, he did not suffer from any sleep issues. I left inspired with courage for my own upcoming cold pond experience, but it was not to be. Sleeting and 2°C. This was not the day to put on my bathing suit and jump into a pond! Even if there was a hot sauna waiting close by.

Earthing

Changes are happening in Western medicine. While some doctors are prescribing cold showers, others are suggesting Earthing. Earthing prescriptions are interesting – they recommend spending 20 minutes each day directly touching the earth, like walking barefoot on grass. One of my young students got so excited about this technique that after learning about it in my on-line after-school program, he ran outside, took off his shirt, and lay down on the ground for 20 minutes. His mother, peering out the front bay window, was puzzled. This student is also the one who, when his mom got impatient at a stoplight, said, *"Maybe you should join Dr. Petry's meditation class with me."* He was 9 years old!

Dr. Tracy Latz, a psychiatrist, is committed to an integrated approach to wellness. She talks about Earthing as a therapeutic practice in her psychiatric work, seminars, and online courses. She sees it as a strong tool in her healing approach, helping her patients reduce their anxiety, boost their mood, and connect into the natural world.

What does Earthing do?

Earthing, also called grounding with the Earth, has been shown to improve sleep, reduce pain, reduce stress, activate the digest and rest system, and speed wound healing. Being in contact with the Earth's surface is good for you and for thousands of years was a natural part of everyday life. In the past, people had direct contact with the Earth and the Earth with people through clothing and shoes made from natural fibers. Your modern life is drastically different, and your body is affected in negative ways.

Your body naturally creates billions of positively charged free radicals, or reactive oxygen species (ROS), every day. These troublemakers can build up and harm your tissues and organs. Earthing allows the Earth's abundant negatively charged free electrons to enter your body, balancing out the positive free radicals and preventing potential damage.

Over 18 years of research shows two major changes when you are grounded. First, there is less inflammation, which is linked to many chronic illnesses and pain. Second, there is a well-regulated circadian system, your body's internal clock that affects things like sleep, body temperature, and hormone secretion cycles within a 24-hour period. In simple terms, Earthing makes your body work better and stay healthier.

If you live in an area (perhaps a concrete jungle) where it is difficult for you to get outside and stroll barefoot in grass or sand, head online to one of several websites that now offer many indoor grounding/earthing products.

Forest Bathing

Natural activities now labeled as *"therapeutic"* were once innate, requiring no interventions. The current need for therapeutic measures arises from a shift away from these ways of life. That is the case with *"forest bathing,"* the act of spending time in nature, typically a forest or wooded area, to experience its healing effects. It has become well regarded as a natural remedy that brings about improvements in human physical and mental health.

Forest bathing, known as shinrin yoku in Japanese, began in the 1980's in Japan as a remedy for elevated levels of work-related stress, It has since gained popularity globally for its effectiveness. Studies have found it to decrease blood pressure, activate the parasympathetic system, deactivate the body's Fight or Flight response, decrease cortisol concentrations related to stress reactions in the body, and increase immune function. The most important benefit, for many people, is the reported decrease in negative moods.

Walking around in the woods seems easy enough – no directions needed. Not quite. Forest bathing does have its nuances, as these easy-to-follow steps reveal:

1. **Electronics** – Leave your electronics behind or turn them off.

2. **Silence is Golden** – If with other people, decide in advance whether some talking or whispering is permitted or whether complete silence is preferred. Your primary allies in this experience are other elements of nature – trees, plants, bird song, even leaves rustling beneath your feet. Other humans are secondary.

3. **Choose a natural setting** – Select a forest or wooded area with an abundance of trees and natural elements. Forest bathing is not a hike or intended for exercise. It is an immersive experience in nature that requires you to slow down and engage your senses.

By doing so, you are able to experience the therapeutic benefits of the natural environment.

4. **Set an Intention** – Direct your thoughts in a clear, focused way to increase the likelihood of your hoped-for experience becoming real. An example of your intention could be, *"As I move throughout the forest, I am open and receptive to experiencing nature in mutually beneficial ways."* The intention adds a layer of purpose to the practice, allowing you to appreciate and absorb the benefits of the forest bathing experience more fully. It also guides your subsequent actions; the intention above would mean you would walk more softly on the earth, ask the flower for permission before you pick it, lean against a tree with thanks, verbalize or just silently send kind thoughts to the beauty around you.

5. **Mindful Presence** – Bring your mind to the present moment. As you do this, all six of your senses will become engaged. Your awareness of smells, textures, colors, and sounds will increase. You can activate your senses further by running your fingers across the bark of a tree, bending down to smell a flower, listening intently to rustling leaves, or noticing the sun casting light up ahead on the path.

6. **Mindful Breathing** – Become aware of your breath to help you stay in the present moment. You may choose to deepen your inhale with long slow rhythmic breaths. Imagine you are breathing in the purity of nature and letting go of the stress and hardships of the day.

7. **Reflect** – Find a comfortable place to sit and reflect on your experience. You have been moving slower as you continued your forest bathing experience. You have been moving along slowly and now it is time to stop, allowing your autonomic nervous system to reset. Notice how your inside world matches the calm and peaceful outside world.

8. **Completion** – Conclude your time in nature by expressing gratitude for the gift of this experience. Acknowledge your connection with your natural surroundings in whatever way resonates with you. To receive the full benefits of a forest bathing experience, two hours is the recommended duration.

Paula's Story

I was living in upstate New York and signed up for a half-day workshop about trees. There were seven of us, all women interested in connecting more deeply with nature. After speaking, the workshop presenter gave us our first assignment. *"Go find your tree and begin to communicate with it. There will be just the right tree for you."*

She handed us a 3" x 5" index card with the how-to instructions. We headed off in different directions, thank goodness. I did not want to chat with a tree with someone next to me.

I quickly spotted my tree, a gigantic eastern white pine, on the opposite side of the meadow. Confidently I crossed the field to arrive at the tree. I had miscalculated. The tree was not interested, at all, in my visit. I sensed that my tree was behind the pine tree and made my way to a small grove of trees.

The spot felt right, even cozy, with zillions of pine needles on the forest floor, giving it a comfortable feeling. As I surmised, my tree was in this small grove. Tall, thin, with a bit of sway mid-way up. The bark was overlapping rectangular strips with a rounded lower edge, a pattern that made it look like a dress. The sunlight gave the tree a pinkish hue.

I followed my written directions. *"Are you, my tree?"* I heard a yes to that question. *"Is it okay if I stand here with you?"* I heard, yes that is okay. Then I began telling the tree the ways we were alike, both tall and thin with a bit of back sway. I shared how I appreciated its unique beauty and loved the pink tint. The longer I stayed the more connected I felt, I even got a bit light-headed.

I heard the sound of a Tibetan bowl, signifying that my 30 minutes were up. As I turned around, magic happened. I saw shooting strings of sparkly white fine filaments in the middle of the grove, about chest high. This is what I know as Indra's Net, the Hindu and Buddhist description of the universal unifying web. Then I heard, *"Tell our story."*

For a flash of a second, I felt ganged up on. The energy came from the circle of trees, not just one, but all of them. My body took a big drink – a big sigh, a pause. The circle of trees felt alive, and my body felt light. Leaning into what had just happened, I felt humbled by the trees' request. When I returned to the class, I chose not to share my full experience. My sacred moment with a grove of trees was for me to digest and cherish.

"Tell our story!" To tell their story, like any good journalist, I had to learn about my subjects. Not from one source, but through multiple sources. I needed to feel, hear, and see the world through their eyes, as much as possible. I continue to do so.

EXERCISE

Life on planet earth through nature's eyes is quite different than through human eyes. And this is your opportunity to experience the profound healing power and connection with nature for yourself.

1: Reflect on how Nature fits into your toolkit.

If you have a garden, experience working in it barefoot. Communicate out loud or in your mind with a beloved plant or flower. Ask permission, as it was done in the amazing spiritual community Findhorn in Scotland, to cut, trim, or move a plant – creating a symbiotic relationship.

Turn off your electronic devices to reduce distractions and set an intention before going out in nature for a walk. Find the exact right practice from these suggestions to make part of your daily goal of flow. As with everything you've learned, pick the ones you enjoy and will do.

2 : Commune with Your Inner Nature

Nature is an integral part of you, and you are an integral part of it. An effective meditation practice with shamanic origins is one where you journey into your secret garden, the garden of your mind and soul. At **24-7flow.com** you can listen to or download the audio meditation, *Journey into Your Sacred Garden*. This audio serves as a roadmap to accessing your sacred garden, a unique inner sanctuary.

As you venture into this journey, actively shape this inner realm according to your desires. You, and you alone, fill your sacred garden with everything it contains. As such, it is a mirror of aspects of yourself seeking expression. Remember, each facet of nature is alive, and you possess the ability to engage with each. Ask probing questions like *"What is my purpose here?"* or *"What do I deeply yearn for?"* to foster a deeper connection with your true Self.

There is a collective need and yearning to return to the symbiotic relationship the human family once had with the natural world millions of years ago. A return to the time when we were evolving as planetary allies, mutually and consciously relying on each other to survive and thrive.

What would it take to live again in that flow and harmony?

The answer to that question may seem overwhelming but you, through using the techniques in your toolkit, can begin or continue a dialogue with the natural world, knowing that as you do so, you step into even greater flow, internal peace and joy.

Chapter Eight :
The Violet Flame – The Spiritual Science of Transmutation

"The changing of bodies into light and light into bodies,
is very comfortable to the course of nature, which seems
delighted with transmutations."

Isaac Newton

For thousands of years now, religious practices have included repeating sacred words and prayers to help people cope with life's challenges and to become closer to God.

Hindu and Buddhist monks repeat mantras; Catholics repeat the rosary and Jews say the Shema along with other denominational practices. Job 22 : 27-28 states, *"Thou shalt make thy prayer unto him, and he shall hear thee, and thou shalt pay thy vows. Thou shall also decree a thing, and it shall be established unto thee: and the light shall shine upon thy ways".*

In many Native American traditions, fire is seen as an aspect or ray of the sun, and the sacred ceremonial fire that accompanies many Native American traditions and dances is viewed as what non-natives might call *"the endless fire"* or eternal flame. Into the sacred fire went whatever was no longer needed on both the personal and community level.

Using fire as a cleansing or purification practice is ancient, as is the idea of the eternal flame. In these practices, fire is both a physical and a spiritual *'being'* that is to be respected as it corresponds to the flame within you and me.

In the Old Testament in Exodus 3 : 2 Moses is presented with the burning bush, but the bush is not consumed. It is not a physical fire but a spiritual one of transformation. This flame is called the Violet Flame. The Violet Flame was a secret thousands of years old, known only by a few saints and mystics of the East. It is said that Jesus revealed it to his most devoted disciples, and alchemists have been depicted in centuries-old drawings concocting a mixture of a fiery flame.

But what exactly is this Violet Flame?

In each of the chapters of this book, we share the scientific evidence that supports the practice we recommend. For the Violet Flame, the *"science"* is anecdotal evidence provided by thousands of people across centuries of devotional practice. So, I ask you to keep an open mind as I share my own experience and that of others. And I hope you, too, will endeavor to work with the Violet Flame in your own life as its power is truly transcendent.

The Violet Flame is also known as the mercy flame or the flame of freedom and forgiveness. It is associated with the seventh spiritual ray and the Holy Spirit. This sacred fire transmutes lower frequency energy to higher frequency. It can break up blockages within the body, which can lead to improved health. It can also transmute lower frequency thinking and feeling so you can experience better mental health.

The violet color is an important part of this flame. Of all the colors you can see within your visual spectrum, violet has one of the highest vibrational frequencies. This light spans the physical and spiritual realms and stands at a transition point between dimensions.

Leigh's Story

I first learned about the Violet Flame shortly after I met my spiritual teacher, Patricia, when I was 22 years old.

Within months of meeting her, I was fired from my first part-time job as a music therapist. Then, my music therapy internship fell through due to the therapist leaving her position at South Florida State Hospital, where I was to complete my training. In a matter of months, my professional life fell apart. I needed to complete my internship in order to become a registered music therapist. I was upset, depressed, and I felt like a victim.

Patricia suggested I use the Violet Flame to help me find another internship. The first step was to change how I was feeling about the situation. Even though these changes came about due to circumstances beyond my control, I felt like the world was against me, at least my small part of it. The truth was I had not been looking forward to my internship; I was leery of the population at the hospital, and my part-time job had not been what I thought it was going to be. I decided to follow my teacher's guidance and use the Violet Flame.

I sat in a meditative state and used my breath and visualization to work with the Violet Flame. I visualized it pouring into my brain, specifically into my pineal gland, which produces endorphins. I got a picture of the gland (this was in the late 1970's so no internet yet) and I visualized activating it with the Violet Flame.

The visualizations were accompanied by what are called Violet Flame decrees. These are I AM statements like mantras that I repeated in my mind. I did this combination for a couple of months and I began to feel hopeful about finding another internship. It took 6 months to a year before being accepted at an approved location, and what made it more difficult is that I wanted to stay in Miami.

I found out in August that my September internship was not happening, but by the end of October, I was offered an internship starting in the following January at United Cerebral Palsy Association of Miami. One of the interns they'd accepted had pulled out, so they had an opening for me. This was unprecedented and amazing!

I believe it was my use of the Violet Flame that made the difference. I was hooked and continued to work with the Violet Flame. When the current music therapist left at the end of my internship, I was hired full-time as their music therapist. It was my dream job that turned into a 42-year, extremely rewarding career, one where I made life-long friendships.

I have been using the Violet Flame for over 40 years and can personally attest to its effectiveness. Its use has become part of my daily routine and helps keep my frequency level high.

Visualizing this flame around me and within specific trouble areas of my body is a mood enhancer and keeps me focused on transmuting lower frequencies instead of perseverating on my aches and pains.

History

This secret of the Violet Flame was revealed on a mass scale in the 1930's through Guy and Edna Ballard of the I AM movement. They channeled an ascended master named St. Germain who works with the Violet Flame on a higher dimension than the earth plane. This is possible because of the high frequency of the violet color. St. Germain lived on planet earth for many hundreds of years before making his ascension, conquering the cycles of death and rebirth.

Whether you believe that St. Germain became immortal and was channeled through the Ballards, you can still practice using the Violet Flame and judge for yourself if it can be an effective tool for healing.

Although the Violet Flame was revealed in the 1930's to a large audience, the Theosophical Society revealed it back in the late 1800's. The main purpose was to form a universal group dedicated to the study of comparative religion, philosophy, and science. Alice Bailey, a member of the society, wrote about the Violet Flame in the early

1900's, including sharing a Violet Flame decree. Since then, many Violet Flame decrees have been implemented.

Perhaps one of the most well-known proponents of the Violet Flame was trance medium Edgar Cayce, a Baptist Sunday-school teacher, and an early twentieth-century clairvoyant whose trance readings were documented and now reside in the library at the Association for Research and Enlightenment in Virginia Beach, VA.

A humble man, Edgar Cayce gave over fourteen thousand readings. In them, he answered questions about healing, reincarnation, past lives, Atlantis, and the Violet Flame. Most of his readings were to help people heal from various illnesses. In over nine hundred of his readings, he recommended an electrical device, which he called a violet ray machine that emits a violet-colored electrical charge to treat various illnesses such as lethargy, poor circulation, and nervous disorders.

You may wonder how purple gained such prominence. The colors of purple and violet have deep associations with ancient healing practices and spiritual systems. In the ancient Byzantine world, purple dye could only be obtained from a type of sea snail. It was both extremely limited and extremely expensive, and only the wealthiest in society (often royalty) could afford to have purple robes or clothes.

Back in 16th Century England, the first Queen Elizabeth decreed that only members of the royal family should wear purple, so associated was the color with the royal lineage. And it wasn't just clothes. The ancient Egyptians considered the amethyst gem a healing stone that could ward off evil. Bards wrapped in purple sang Homer's Odyssey.

When Pilate's soldiers put the crown of thorns on the head of Jesus, they placed a purple robe on him. This led to purple being an important color in Christian worship. And, as noted earlier, violet has one of the highest vibrational frequencies of the colors you can see in your visual spectrum, spanning the physical and spiritual realms.

How Does It Work?

Quantum physicists would say that when you call on the Violet Flame, it creates a polarity between the nucleus in the atom and the white fire core of the flame.

This is a combination of the negative pole of the nucleus, being matter, and the positive pole of the flame, being spirit. This results in an oscillation or vibration that can break up the density within the problem area of the body. This density is then purified, allowing the electrons to move freely once again, releasing the condition.

Negative energy slows the cycling of your electrons. By using the Violet Flame and raising the vibratory rate of your electrons, you can raise your consciousness and keep yourself in the flow of your day at the highest frequency possible.

As your electrons move faster, you want them to continue to move faster and faster. Keeping up with using the Violet Flame throughout the day can enhance this speed and help you feel more exuberant and raise the feelings of joy and happiness for those around you.

All illnesses, according to Dr. Zhi Gang Sha in his book *"Soul, Mind, Body Medicine"*, are a result of blockages, Dr. Sha explains there are only two types of energy imbalances that can result in sickness. One is too much energy between the cells and the other is not enough energy between the cells. The Violet Flame creates the vibration between the poles of the nucleus, allowing these imbalances to correct themselves.

How to Work with the Violet Flame and Decrees

Violet Flame decrees are often said aloud to accentuate the energy of the power of the spoken word. They are prayers, fiats, mantras, and affirmations. They take the form of a command rather than a request. When you decree, you are directing light into your world, invoking energy from spirit into matter. You are not only using light, but you are also using the power of sound. You know through the research in the Music as Medicine chapter that sound can be the key to physical, emotional, and spiritual healing.

Another technique used while decreeing is to begin the decree at a normal speaking pace and as you repeat it, speed up the pace as well as the tone. Repeating it gives the decree greater power and brings in more light. It can be thought of as a train picking up speed. Increasing the speed should be done naturally, as you feel the energy increasing through the repetition. The flame obeys your spoken words and accelerates according to the tempo. You might automatically pick up the pace as you begin to feel your energy building.

Use of the Violet Flame helps raise your frequency, so it is important to have fun with it! You can be very creative with your visualizations. There are myriad ways to visualize the flame. See it moving in large circles, spirals, figure-eight, waterfalls or lightning. I like to visualize it dancing all around. Each time it lands on something I am visualizing, I sense it picking up the negative or lower frequency energy and transmuting it into a higher vibration. You can use your hands to direct it, perhaps by using a Tai Chi motion or Qi Gong movements. The important thing is to make the practice your own in a way that feels right to you.

If you already love the color purple, you might wear clothes the color of violet or purple to remind you to think of the Violet Flame throughout the day. You can sleep in purple pajamas! Wear your amethyst jewelry against your skin, such as a ring, pendant or anklet. Amethyst gems vibrate at a frequency of the Violet Flame so wearing them can help you stay in the flow. You can put larger amethyst gems in your house or on your altar if you have one to raise the overall frequency in your home.

You can visualize the Violet Flame while out walking and imagine tiny Violet Flames sprouting up from the ground under your feet. You can do this in any situation or task that you complete throughout the day.

When you are sweeping the floor, imagine the flames transmuting the dirt. Do the same when vacuuming. If you can sit in front of a fire, visualize the flames as violet and feel the energy being transmuted as the flames crackle.

Nancy's Story

Nancy is a woman in her seventies who fell and broke one of the bones in her wrist. She was reluctant to have it checked, as she did not think it was broken. She eventually went to an orthopedist and was told it was a transverse distal radius fracture with dorsal angulation.

As soon as she was injured, she began using the Violet Flame. She was told she probably would need surgery but, after working with the Violet Flame, surgery was not required.

Nancy chose a purple wrap around her cast, signifying the Violet Flame. Every time her wrist was painful, she invoked the Violet Flame.

Every time, the pain would lessen and cease. She said it was simply amazing! Each time she went to the doctor, she was told that the wrist was healing beautifully. She feels her use of the Violet Flame was a major factor in avoiding surgery and in her successful healing.

EXERCISE

You can do this exercise at whatever place and time of day works best for you. As much as possible, try to keep your legs and hands uncrossed so you can keep the light and energy flowing freely. Breathe deeply and center in your heart before you begin. You can say a short prayer, asking for unseen assistance from your higher power or your guides or guardian angel.

Concentrate on the words and direct the violet light where you want it to go. Visualize the desired results. Look at a picture of the Violet Flame as a visual aid. As a beginner, say the decrees given below slowly and deliberately and gradually increase the speed as you feel more comfortable. Choose one of the ways from the ideas presented above, to work with the Violet Flame in your daily life.

Choose whatever appeals most to you. Start with a simple I AM decree such as: *"I AM a being of violet fire. I AM the purity God desires."* The term *"I AM"* is another name for God, the *"I AM THAT I AM"* given to Moses. This is an affirmation of the spark of divinity within yourself. Here are others to use. You can also create your own.

I AM the Violet Flame.

I AM the Violet Flame in action in me now.

I AM the Violet Flame, to light alone I bow.

I AM the Violet Flame in mighty cosmic power.

I AM the light of God shining every hour.

I AM the Violet Flame blazing like the sun.

I AM God's sacred power freeing everyone.

As you are saying these decrees, you can direct the Violet Flame to any area of your body. Visualize the flame surrounding your heart or your thyroid or any problem area.

Other Ways to Use the Violet Flame Decrees

By now, you must be getting the idea that you can incorporate your use of the Violet Flame in almost any situation throughout your day!

It is a wonderful way to stay in the flow 24/7. This is a good example of the combination of science and spiritual practice. Making a difference in your own world can have a positive affect for others. Your friends will be asking you what you are doing to make you so lighthearted and joyful.

The Violet Flame is one of the missing keys in your life to create improved health, better relationships, and a general feeling of well-being. Here are decrees that you can customize to spread healing and light to others and the world:

O Violet Flame, Come, Violet Flame

O Violet Flame, come, Violet Flame,

Now blaze and blaze and blaze!

O Violet Flame, come, Violet Flame,

To raise and raise and raise!

(Repeat verse between the following endings)

1. *The earth and all thereon (3x)*

2. *The children and their teachers (3x)*

3. *The plants and elemental creatures (3x)*

4. *The air, the sea, the land (3x)*

5. *Make all to understand (3x)*

6. *Bless all by Omri-Tas' hand (3x)*

7. *I AM, I AM, I AM the fullness of God's plan fulfilled right now and forever (3x)*

Omri-Tas is an ascended master who intensifies the action of the Violet Flame so that is why his name is invoked in this decree. These decrees have been published by the Summit Lighthouse *(Light bearers of the World, Unite! 2005, Summit Publications, Inc.)*

There are many Violet Flame meditations incorporating decrees available on YouTube. Feel free to try different ones to see which you want to incorporate into your day.

To use the Violet Flame, all you have to do is ask.

You might often read about things you would like to do but don't put them into practice. There are many unseen beings around you and great spiritual figures there to help you. Think of them as your spiritual support system. However, they cannot interfere with your free will. Therefore, you need to call on them for assistance. The same is true for working with the Violet Flame.

May the Violet Flame empower you, and through you, empower the light of love, healing and joy to reach to all those in need.

Chapter Nine : Closing Down Your Day

"You had a peaceful day during the day and a peaceful sleep at night, that's what real wealth is!"

Mehmet Murat ildan

Now that you have maintained a high frequency as much as possible throughout the day by using the exercises given, it is time to wind down and complete the day's flow.

It seems like time moves faster than it used to and before you know it, the day is over, and it is time to prepare for the end of the day. Maybe you have never thought about planning the end of the day, but it can be part of living a conscious life.

For much of your life, maybe you have rushed around like a wild person at the end of the day, trying to get done what you planned on doing earlier in the day but didn't get done.

Maybe you have a routine of getting kids to bed or doing paperwork from your job and by the time you get this done, you are exhausted and just fall into bed. Or maybe you drink a few glasses of wine or some other alcoholic beverage and blankly watch something on TV or mindlessly scroll through social media.

After all that evening chaos or brainless vegging out, you get into bed and what happens? You cannot fall asleep!

You feel exhausted and yet, you are wide awake! Maybe you have restless legs, or you just cannot shut your mind off. You do not know whether to stay in bed or get up and make yourself useful by doing those dishes you did not finish or maybe reading a book will put you to sleep. Even though you get up and try some of these activities, when you get back in bed you still cannot fall asleep... or maybe you fall asleep but wake up just several hours later and then cannot go back to sleep!

All of this may be avoided if you take a step back and begin to think proactively about sleep preparations and how to end the day by continuing a flow that leads to successful sleep.

One of the most important parts of this plan is when to go to sleep.

It is important to go to bed at approximately the same time every night and wake up at the same time. This cannot always be done but it should be the rule rather than the exception. Having consistent bed and wake times allows your internal circadian rhythm to operate at an optimal level. Research has shown it helps you fall asleep easier and stay asleep.

Most doctors recommend you should get at least seven hours of sleep per night. Once you operate in a flow state throughout much of the day, you may not require as much. It is up to you to determine what is best for you. Whatever you decide, if you need to get up at 5:00am, you will need to go to bed by 10:00pm to get seven hours of sleep.

Adjust your times based on the number of hours you need and stick to it as much as possible.

After a couple of weeks, you will begin to notice a difference in how quickly you fall asleep and the quality of your sleep. This practice includes weekends and other days you don't necessarily need to get up early. Once you have the pattern developed, as with anything else, you may have days where you do not follow it.

If you are a person who likes to take naps during the day, you need to be aware this may throw off your sleep schedule. It is recommended you keep your naps to not more than 30 minutes. Longer naps can leave you feeling groggy and may interfere in your ability to have a good sleep at night.

It is also recommended you not take a nap too late in the afternoon. A family member of mine always took a nap once he arrived home from work and needed to be awakened to eat dinner. He chronically had trouble falling to sleep. It was a joke in the family that he always looked tired!

Other planning tips in preparation for sleep include not drinking caffeine after mid-afternoon and not drinking alcohol in the hour before you plan on going to bed. You may think alcohol makes you drowsy and indeed it does. However, it can lower your sleep quality so it is best to have it with dinner, which should be at least a few hours before going to bed. The last tip is to disconnect your devices an hour before you go to bed because they can suppress your natural production of melatonin.

Leigh's Approach

I like to watch TV in the evening, but I avoid anything that could be upsetting. I have my favorite comedies and dramas and I also like documentaries or other entertainment shows. I make sure to turn off the TV forty-five minutes to an hour before I plan on going to sleep.

To prepare for sleep I read uplifting or inspiring articles and stories or I might even read several chapters in the current book I keep on the nightstand, or simply a couple of inspirational sentences. Some evenings I take a bath and read while in the tub, and I find that adding essential oils or other ingredients conducive to sleep can be helpful.

To relax my body, I perform a few stretches and Qi Gong exercises before getting into bed. These types of movements calm the nervous system and aid in relaxing the body. I often combine these gentle movements with some breathing exercises and mindfulness. If I don't feel like going through all the exercises, I simply do some deep breathing combined with neck stretches and overhead stretches.

Lastly, I enjoy sitting on the edge of my bed and humming or singing a soft chant. In yoga, the practice of humming is called "bee breath". One way to do this is to take a deep breath and while exhaling, create a humming or buzzing sound at the back of your throat. To enhance this as bedtime practice, press the outer folds of your ears against your ears so your ears are plugged. This amplifies the internal buzzing sound and brings you inward as you work towards breaking away from outside stimulation.

With this preparation in place, I finally get in bed! All of these practices that form my routine for closing down my day feel effortless and, once in bed, I meditate, often using the violet flame meditation to transmute any negative situations I might have encountered during the day. I combine that with healing visualizations if there is any area of my body where I feel discomfort or pain. I silently affirm my intention for a deep, restful night's sleep.

I often fall asleep during my meditation. This is a fine and lovely way to enter the sleep state, and is an ideal way to enter into sleep.

Paula's Approach

My sleep routine requires a few elements. First is a hot shower, about one hour before bedtime to help relax my body. The second is closing all the curtains and shades, with preferably not a spot of light coming into my room. In the winter I love to have the room cold with blankets piled on top, helping me feel safe and cozy. As I cocoon myself in for a good night's sleep, I say words of gratitude about the day. I mention in my mind who and what I am grateful for, regardless of what happened during the day. My gratitude element of my sleep preparation sets my heart in an open and receptive state. I also say the Lord's Prayer.

If I need to resolve a matter of the heart, I set a dream intention, asking that it resolve in my dreamtime. My dream journal sits on my nightstand along with my phone, silenced in airplane mode. I rarely set an alarm, because if I'm startled awake in the morning it scrambles up my day.

Create Your Own Routine

It is important to take stock of your physical, mental and emotional states as you prepare for bed and use whatever techniques you like that help you feel balanced, calm and contented.

If you get into bed and cannot seem to relax, get up and do some light exercises to try to calm your body and mind. Perhaps an eye mask would be helpful. Research has shown it is important to have your room as dark as possible. You might have electronic devices that emit light or even blink. These can be very distracting and can interfere with quality sleep. They also can prevent you waking up before your alarm because your bedroom is getting some light coming from the rising sun. This can be a particular problem when daylight saving occurs.

With the techniques listed in this chapter, you can have a deep sleep that allows for rejuvenation and dream revelation. Healthy sleep helps the body stave off diseases and keeps the mind alert. Keeping the functions of your body flowing including the respiratory, circulatory and hormonal systems is dependent upon quality sleep. Preparing to fall asleep in a conscious manner can keep you in the flow 24/7!

EXERCISE

Think about how you normally close down your day. Most likely, as discussed in the beginning of this chapter, you might fall into bed exhausted from work or caretaking others. Perhaps you get a late-night news fix and then try to calm your mind and free it of worrisome thoughts so you can fall asleep. Perhaps you eat dinner very late and find you need to take antacids just to feel physically comfortable enough to fall asleep. If you share your bed with another, you are sharing energy.

If your sleeping partner is restless at night or snores or otherwise disrupts your sleep, take the time to talk together about how to create a routine that helps both of you feel restored through a good night's sleep. It may not be possible every night, especially if you have young children, but together you can agree on how to create as optimal an environment as possible,

Now that you've thought about why you might not get the restorative sleep you need most nights, jot down a new routine for yourself. Put on your plan what you can control, not other people's behavior. If you can wear small headphones to bed, you might want to fall asleep to white noise or a soothing meditation. There are plenty of products now available in the marketplace to help you create a bedroom and sleep routine that keeps light and noise from disrupting your sleep.

Add making sure you are only breathing through your nose at night to your list and, if not, get the sleep tape mentioned in the chapter on the vagus nerve to help you make sure you can do that. After a few nights you should notice improved sleep just from that one change. Remember it is a process of trial and error as you not only adjust to a new routine but also experiment with which techniques help you the best. Ending your day in a calm, flow state, means you'll be ready to step into 24-7 flow when you wake.

Chapter Ten :
Into the Matrix – What Your
Dreams Reveal

"Our ability to regulate our emotions each day is key to what we call emotional IQ – and this depends on getting sufficient REM sleep night after night after night."

Matthew Walker

Have you seen those Matrix movies? You know – the ones in which there is a reality behind the reality that is invisible to most?

While those are science fiction films, there is a matrix of a sort in your inner life, and it is accessible to you once the conscious mind sleeps and you enter the field of dreams. You now understand the importance of closing your day in a way that supports healthy, restorative sleep. You have learned how to prepare to fall asleep in a conscious manner. Reading inspirational messages, expressing gratitude, electronics off, light stretches, and deep breathing all calm your nervous system. This sets the stage for the next day's flow. As you nestle into bed and the lights softly fade, you are most prepared to benefit from another critical element of your sleep regimen, REM sleep plus dreaming.

Now get ready. You're about to delve into the most mysterious part of sleep, the REM stage – dreamtime. Maybe you've wondered why you dream and what your dreams mean? Maybe you think you don't dream as you have no memory of dreams upon awakening? But dream you do. And learning how to work with your dreams gives you another powerful tool for your toolkit, one that provides access to that most mysterious part of your psyche – your subconscious, the hidden driver behind so much of what you believe about yourself.

So why learn to work with your dreaming mind? Is it truly so vital to enter REM sleep and dream? Yes! If you are chronically sleep deprived, the flow state as we have presented is not achievable. Quality sleep and consistent REM dream time are essential.

Life Enhancement Prescription:

REM Sleep *plus* Dreaming Benefits!

- Enhanced Memory

- Inspired Creativity

- Release of Toxic Emotional Residue built up during Waking Hours

- Strengthened Immune System

- Strengthened Interconnectivity with the Brain

- Assists in Healing and Releasing Trauma

- Deepened Emotional Intelligence

- Increased Self-Knowledge

Do you need this prescription? Do you need more sleep? If so, you are not alone. According to the Council on Aging in the US, about 30% of all adults have symptoms of insomnia, with 11% having chronic insomnia. And the Centers for Disease Control and Prevention show that 1 in 3 adults report not getting enough rest or sleep every day.

If you are chronically missing out on the body's natural power boost, keep reading. Without the benefits of quality REM, you will experience a level of anxiety and possibly depression that is solely due to the lack of sleep. You will also experience misfired thoughts, misread emotional cues, and the frustration that comes with being mentally flat, due to the lack of creativity pouring into your waking hours.

If this is you, before you head to the medicine cabinet or a therapist, understand that every tool in your toolkit helps you sleep. This chapter adds another tool. When you use this tool along with the ones you've already learned, your sleep will improve; staying in flow will be easier.

Here Comes the Science!

On the premise that a little bit of knowledge goes a long way, let's review what happens during your sleep time. Typically, you cycle through four distinct stages of sleep multiple times during a night's rest. On average, a complete sleep cycle lasts around 90 to 110 minutes. Throughout the night, you may experience four to six cycles of these stages, with the duration and distribution of each stage varying. Each cycle has its unique contribution to our health and well-being.

The stages are labeled, N1, N2 etc. The N stands for non-REM which indicates the importance of the REM stage, all other stages are labeled describing them as not REM. Let's look at each stage.

Stage 1 : N1

You are dosing off, not fully relaxed and your brain activity begins to change from an active alpha brain wave to a theta brain wave. This stage normally lasts just one to seven minutes. If you then go into deep slumber, you typically won't cycle back into this stage.

Stage 2 : N2

In any given night you will spend about half of your sleep time in this stage. Your body temperature drops, you might reach for a blanket, your muscles relax, and you have slowed breathing and heart rate. The first Stage 2 cycle lasts between 10 and 25 minutes.

Stage 3 : N3

This is deep sleep. Have you ever tried waking someone up who is in a deep sleep? Or were woken yourself? You know how difficult and disorienting it is for the sleeper. It's like waking a bear up from deep slumber. This stage is the most essential for body restoration, allowing for tissue repair and cell regeneration, and immune system strengthening; it also contributes to insightful thinking. This stage lasts from 20 to 60 minutes.

Stage 4 : Rapid Eye Movement (REM)

The REM (Rapid Eye Movement) stage is significantly different than the other three stages. While in the initial stages (1 through 3), the body progressively becomes less active; during REM sleep, the brain becomes highly active. It is during this stage that you experience your most vivid and sometimes bizarre dreams. Thanks to modern medical technology, particularly neuroimaging techniques like MRI (Magnetic Resonance Imaging), neuroscientists have been able to gain insight into the particulars of REM sleep, unraveling its inner workings and significance in the sleep cycle.

Picture yourself in a deep sleep, reclining inside an MRI machine, a device designed to reveal the inner workings of your body and brain through magnetic imaging. As you lie there, the EEG records your brain activity. It reveals that you've entered the N3 sleep stage, characterized by slow 7 to 14Hz brain waves, a decreased heart rate, and relaxed muscles. Other brain centers show minimal to no activity, indicating a deep state of slumber.

Now imagine you begin to dream, leaving the N3 stage and entering the REM stage. For fun, pause a moment and recall a vivid dream. Remember the colors, movements, smells, sounds, emotions. The who, what, and where of the dream. Now imagine you are still inside the MRI machine – dreaming your dream. Imagine you can see the images of your brain projected onto the monitor and the readouts of other body indicators.

This is what you would be seeing on the monitors:

1. Your brain wave is in an awakened state of theta or beta.

2. Your heart rate has increased.

3. Your eyes rapidly move back and forth, the only area of your body not paralyzed.

4. You notice areas of your brain lighting up, based on what is happening in your dream. When you are chasing someone, the motor cortex lights up. The brain centers would include:

   a. Visual spatial center

   b. Motor cortex

   c. Autobiographical – Hippocampus - memory

   d. Emotional memory

5. Your nerve pathways are activated – those that prevent muscles from moving.

6. You then notice an area of your brain that is notably offline:

   a. Prefrontal cortex, the brain's CEO – logic and reasoning

7. You later learn that the stress related chemical, norepinephrine – is offline as well.

Isn't it fascinating how your body is wired for the world of dreams?

First when you dream, your body hits the pause button on movement. It's like your own built-in safety feature to prevent you from acting out the scenarios. On rare occasions this function does not work properly and can result in what is called sleepwalking.

Secondly, your brain's CEO, that which provides logic and reason, is taking a break. This allows you to do all sorts of things that wouldn't happen in real life. Normally when you are frightened, e.g. someone is chasing you down a dark alley, your brain releases a stress hormone called norepinephrine. But during dreamtime, this hormone is switched off, not startling you awake. Not turned off is your memory center, allowing for prior experiences and emotional content to be woven into the dream space.

There is no question, you are designed to dream. But why?

The researcher and author Matthew Walker explored this question in his book, *Why We Sleep: Unlocking the Power of Sleep and Dreams*. His conclusion is that REM sleep plus dreaming has the primary role of removing the painful sting out of the day's emotionally challenging experiences.

He postulates that dreams primarily exist to help you digest your emotional world. A mechanism that has helped humanity navigate increasingly more complex brain structures, social dynamics, and emotional landscapes over the past 2 million years.

Daniel's Story

A good example of the power of dreams to resolve inner turmoil comes from one of my clients. Daniel came to see me shortly after I had finished my year-long Jungian dream analysis course. I was eager to apply my knowledge. He wanted to resolve his love relationships. He was not married at the time and the woman he had been dating had broken up with him.

Several days before his first session, a type of mantra kept running through his mind, *"love cannot be found by seeking".* In talking with him about this, he concluded that love is found not by seeking but by *"staying on the road, through commitment".* (A profound message for all of us.) At the end of the session, I directed him to expect to receive a message about his mantra during dreamtime and to set that intention.

When I saw him next, seven days later, he had four recorded dreams; when he woke up from the dream, he would use his phone to record the dream and then fall back to sleep. He shared it with me.

"I am on a rooftop at dinner or perhaps lunch with lots of people. I am the host and I'm trying to take a team photo. There are four speakers, two of the speakers are playing songs and the other two speakers are my own. They are trying to make music with their equipment, but I want to use my own equipment. I heard the song, You Are Still the One, playing. I was wearing a green shirt with a white and green logo on my left side.

"There's a lovely lady and man at the bar and she's coming to me, and she said, "You look like my father". I am taking off my hat and said, "I don't look like your father". Now it's time for the group photo. The group had gotten very large, extending way beyond the room.

"There was a photographer taking the photos. In the first photo I was not visible. So, for the second photo I straightened up. But I kept asking for more photos to be taken. There were no good photos. I was not happy with any of the photos; I was never visible in them. Two men are on the right of me, and they are complaining about having to stand there while more and more photos are taken. One said, "Why does he get to tell them to take more photos?" I responded, "The photographer only does this because I am paying the bill. I invited and I am paying, that is why I am the boss." Then I woke up.

I first responded by acknowledging how brave he was to allow his subconscious to come to the surface through dreamtime, and to bring the content into the session. Both signs that my client had the fortitude and determination to resolve long-standing emotional issues.

When asked, he reported that his feelings were mostly neutral but at the end, he felt powerful but not happy. As we discussed the dream, he frequently said, *"Oh My God".* He felt his dream accurately portrayed an aspect of himself that was hidden, even from himself.

We talked about the themes in his dream, i.e. the relationship with and between money and power, effect of his male lineage's belief system around money, power and women, what his visibility with his father had been and with others as a child, and who would he be without money and power.

By the next session a pain in his left side had disappeared and he was feeling lighter. His dreams continued to help him become conscious of what had been centuries of the adage *"What's love got to do with it?"* In his lineage, on both his maternal and paternal sides, as expressed in the dream, love did not have anything to do with marriage. Marriage was about money and power.

As I worked with him, in one of his sessions a book appeared in my mind's eye, ***The Book of Love***, in a beautiful red/orangish font; he was to be its author. We talked about the belief that some people, particularly spiritual seekers, come into this lifetime to bring a new consciousness into their lineage. That felt like the truth to him.

Paula's Dream Story

I have many dreams I could share but here is one that brought me a greater understanding about myself and my life at the time. My dream was shortly after the ending of a romantic relationship.

A black horse came galloping full speed moving from right to left way out in front of me. There was a tiny black figure on top, not a human shape but like a gingerbread man shape – a thin cut out of a person.

The horse suddenly came to a full stop, sending the man overhead. The horse then trampled him – presumably to death. The horse then ran towards me, closer and closer until we were eyeball to eyeball. It was subtle but it felt like the horse was pleased with himself. I then woke up. My heart was racing, and I felt unsettled.

I was in a dream study group at the time of the dream. I shared the dream and asked for help interpreting it. As it often goes, no one else found it difficult to decipher. I was so detached from my feelings about the breakup, particularly my anger, that it took others to help me understand my dream.

In the dream, I was both the observer and the horse. My ability to trample someone to death doesn't suggest anything about my conscious life and character. It just means I am not always aware of and able to process my strong feelings. I did that work in my dreamtime.

Waking up while dreaming helped me to further digest its meaning. I had two other dreams, equally prophetic, about the relationship. Together they helped me regain emotional balance about what had been a difficult time in my life.

Setting Intentions

You've learned about the importance of setting an intention to shape the course of your day. You can apply that same concept to your REM sleep and dream time. Set a dream intention before you go to sleep. It can be as simple as asking for assistance in resolving that which is weighing heavily on your heart.

However, remember intention is not expectation. Expectation creates anxiety; between expectation and outcome is the potential for disappointment which tenses the body and can block the flow. Allow the dream to come through you.

The REM cycle, that mysterious phase of our 24-hour clock, has entranced the curious minds of humanity for millennia. My fascination with the mysterious realm of REM sleep was reignited during a recent trip to ancient Greece. Standing on the very ground where dreams were once considered potent prescriptions for ailments, I could not help but feel a profound sense of awe and curiosity.

It was August 2023; the day I landed in Athens it was 114°F; I hid out in my hotel room for a couple of days. When it dropped to 100°F, I eagerly joined a tour of the Parthenon, the majestic Greek temple dedicated to the goddess Athena.

Before we began our climb, and as we stood on the southwest side of the Parthenon, the tour guide pointed to an area above, and explained that we were looking at the remains of the Asklepion of Athens, the sanctuary built in honor of the gods Asclepius and Hygeia. The asclepias is a healing temple. Fascinated I listened closely, remembering the mention of sleep temples in my Jungian dream analysis classes.

Asclepias comes from Asclepius, who was the first doctor-demigod in Greek mythology and is said to be the son of the god Apollo and a mortal woman. His genealogy is overly complex. He was a powerful healer and people would flock to his temples for spiritual, mental, emotional and physical reasons. Today's medical symbol of a serpent wrapped around a staff is modeled from the staff that Asclepius was said to use.

One of the practices in use at the asclepias was called incubation, also known as *'temple sleep'*. In this process, patients would go to sleep in special quarters with the desire to be visited by Asclepius. During this sleep time, the patient would set the intention to have a dream that contained the prescription needed to cure their ailment. In the morning, they would describe their dream to the priest who would interpret their dream and prescribe the remedy.

Regardless of whether you believe the prescription came from Asclepius, angelic forces, or the person's own inner wisdom, one thing remains clear, dreams contain important information. This fact has until recently largely faded from our modern life. Due to the rise of scientific inquiry, priority has been given to what is tangible and measurable – dreams are illusive and subjective.

This short dream, from my Jungian dream analysis course, is the best example of what I mean. The dreamer was in a forest, he walked to a tree and urinated. As he turned to leave, he noticed ants racing over to the pool of urine. To understand this dream, I thought about what

I know about the nature of ants. Think about what happens if you leave candy out on a countertop. Ants love sugar. What is the importance of urine and sugar? The dreamer was being warned that he has diabetes. He had too much sugar in his urine. His dream alerted him to what might be a serious health issue, one that his dream empowered him to address.

Importance is given today to technology and that which adds to production outputs. The sacred and mysterious have given way to the secular. Contemplation is less valued than busyness. In general, while dreams add depth to our lives, the modern world is interested in what is concrete on the surface.

Dreams and Contemplation – Things to Consider

- Honoring your dreams aligns you with your divine design.

- Recognizing truths about yourself brings an inner sense of peace and restfulness.

- Dreams are manifestations of subconscious content, and by recording and reflecting on them, valuable insights are gained.

- By contemplating dream content, you bring subconscious material into conscious awareness, reducing stress and promoting relaxation.

- Engaging with the creative aspects of dreams fosters expanded creativity.

- Dreams provide specific answers and insights.

- Sharing dreams with loved ones enhances intimacy, serving as a touchstone for understanding each other's inner worlds.

- To ensure openness and respect, it is important to stay non-judgmental and allow the dreamer to be his own witness.

There are several categories or types of dreams. You may have heard of the term *Lucid Dreaming*. Lucid dreaming is simply being aware that you are dreaming while you are dreaming. You realize that you are in a dream as both the observer and the doer. You may then choose to direct the action in the dream, realizing how expansive your inner world truly is.

Dreams show you aspects of your *self*, your patterns of thinking, your behaviors and hidden emotions. Be curious rather than judgmental. I want to leave you with a dream and a question for you to ponder. In my dream my daughter Alexandra was hovering above me. I could see her face so perfectly, very much as she was when she transitioned. She was surrounded by milky white flowing energy; I felt a radiance. We smiled at each other for several seconds and then I woke up. I had so much peace inside of me.

Many people believe loved ones come and visit us during dreamtime. I do. They come to be with us, give advice, share their feelings, and show their support during challenging times. The more open we are to receiving their visits, the more likely it will occur.

A friend of mine, Beatriz, had such a dream. She shared that one of her wishes was to be comforted after the loss of a family member by dreaming with them. Her wish came true. It was 2001, her aunt, then 64 years old passed away very suddenly during a surgery procedure.

She was dear to the family, having lived in their household through all her childhood, teenager and young adult years. It was a very upsetting death because her aunt had been very optimistic about the surgery's success.

Beatriz's Story

I had this dream the same night my aunt transitioned. In the dream she came to my room in my parent's big house where I used to live in Brazil. When she entered the room, I asked what she was doing there (in the dream I reminded myself that she was dead).

She said in a confused way that she was still living in the basement and that she wasn't very happy with all that happened. In the dream, she blamed my parents for what happened but didn't explain to me the reason. My father was a physician, so this made sense to me.

After I had the dream, I thought about what it meant. In the dream, my aunt was in my parents' house, but instead of being on the top floor where she used to live, she was in the basement. I interpreted the basement as symbolizing the underworld. It seemed to me that she was still here on the Earth plane, trying to understand what happened because her death was sudden and unexpected. It felt like she came to me seeking an explanation. Her unhappiness was related to the tense relationship she had with my mother.

EXERCISE

I invite you to keep a *dream journal*. This is the most assured way to benefit from your dreams. Remember, what we pay attention to, we get more of. By paying attention to your dreamtime – it will expand.

1. Acquire a bound dream journal – expect privacy in it being bound. Place it on your nightstand with a pen.

2. Take a small piece of paper and write the words *Set Intention* on it. Put it on top of your pillow, as a reminder.

3. Place a full glass of water next to your dream journal. When you go to bed, drink half of the glass of water. Tell yourself that when you wake up from your dream you will drink the other half glass of water.

4. When you wake up, write down your dream immediately. Know your dream will feel wispy and will fade quickly. Jot down the main visual clues and fill in the narrative after.

5. As soon as you can, write down all the details you remember.

Guidelines to Process Your Dreams

1. Silently read your dream and make sure you have included all the details.

2. Read your dream out loud. You may notice nuances by doing this.

3. Review your dream's meaning, imagining that you are everyone in the dream.

4. Reflect on your emotions. Pay attention to the emotions you experienced during the dream. Emotions can provide valuable clues about what your subconscious is trying to communicate.

5. Consider all aspects of the dream, e.g. colors, location, positioning of one thing in relation to another, the size of the objects or people in the dream. All details are relevant.

6. Dreams are not straightforward. They are layered in symbolism. Words can have double meaning. For example, in one of my client's dreams, there were 4 speakers, as in audio boxes. But in the context of the dream, we agreed that the speakers represented people - who were speaking.

7. Resist relying on a dream dictionary. Use it sparingly, perhaps looking up the spiritual meaning of a symbol you don't recognize in your dream.

8. Examine the metaphysical nature of the main element(s) in your dream, their beingness and connections. What is the element's core nature? Think back to the earlier dream a client shared in which the core nature of ants provided the clue to understanding the dream's full meaning.

I urge you to explore the depths of your dreams with curiosity. Begin by setting a nightly intention before you sleep and invest in a journal to document your dreams. Consider joining an online class or community-based dream group.

By engaging in the exchange of dreams, you'll uncover universal human themes, enriching your understanding of human experience and your own inner life. Working regularly with your dreams will allow you to cleanse your emotional and mental energy fields each day so you can step into flow more easily.

Your dreaming mind provides a fascinating realm of discovery. Cherish the treasures you will find within.

Chapter Eleven :
The Ebb and Flow of Commitment

"Life is a succession of lessons which must be lived to be understood."
Ralph Waldo Emerson

Living in flow means that you have acquired the ability to be aware of who you are being at any given moment. You have acquired the ability to self-correct and take full responsibility for what you create, both the glorious and the dreadful.

You are able to be present in the moment, which connects you with your intuition, making decisions from a quality vantage point. To develop the ability to live in flow is a conscious awakening process. You now have the tools you need to continue your journey.

This journey will be the most exhilarating adventure you will ever embark on. It is complete with aha moments of amazing insight, synchronicities that defy all probability, moments of bliss and feelings of being one with all beings. It leads to mental and emotional freedom that is otherwise unattainable. It is a freedom that awakens your compassion, empathy, creativity, awe and wonder. It ignites your courage to be vulnerable and authentic to whatever may come. The ordinary becomes extraordinary through a perspective that says life is good to me and I am good to life.

However wonderful that all is, and how easily you might have read through this book and tried the practices to follow, know that sustaining the practices in your toolkit might not be so easy.

More than likely, you will fall away, push aside your toolkit, perhaps even forget what is inside, and go about your busy life, only to be drawn back in because your inner world needs you. You recognize that you feel better about yourself and others when you consciously tend to your heart, mind, and body. So, as you embark on and continue your journey, embrace ebb and flow and know that is part of the process.

You might ask what is my end game? If I knew where all of this is leading, I could increase my odds of staying on track. You are right, knowing the how and the what gives meaning to your actions, which generates better outcomes.

The Scale of Consciousness (also known as the Map of Consciousness) by the late Dr. David Hawkins, founder of The Institute for Spiritual Research, is a visual to help you imagine your journey. It is a developmental ladder, expressed in frequencies, that shows the contrast between people's paradigms of existence, the lens through which they interpret all their experiences.

For example, looking at the foot of the table, an individual consumed by fear has high anxiety, is withdrawn, and fears punishment. Going up the ladder of consciousness, as that same individual evolves, emotions or states of being like courage, acceptance, and love become accessible. The higher you go, the more positive and empowering your emotions become.

LEVEL	CALIBRATION	DESCRIPTION
Enlightenment	700 - 1,000	Powerful Inspiration
Peace	600	Bliss, Illumination
Joy	540	Compassion, Effortless
Love	500	Caring, Inclusive
Reason	400	Logic, Science, Math
Acceptance	350	Calm, Balanced, Objective
Willingness	310	Can-do, Open-minded
Neutrality	250	Flexible, Non-judgmental
Courage	200	Determination, Optimism
Pride	175	Arrogance, Haughtiness
Anger	150	Resentment, Irritation, Frustration
Desire	125	Greed, Lust, Insatiability
Fear	100	Anxiety, Nervousness
Grief	75	Sadness, Despondency
Apathy	50	Despair, Hopelesness
Guilt	30	Deep Regret
Shame	20	Self-hatred

POWER / FORCE

TRUTH / FALSEHOOD

The Scale of Consciousness (also known as the Map of Consciousness)
by the late Dr. David Hawkins, founder of The Institute for Spiritual Research

The Scale of Consciousness relates to flow, your toolkit and staying motivated in important ways. First, it is easy to understand that life increasingly moves into a state of flow as you move up the ladder. The higher your energy field vibrates, the more flow you experience. Second, all the tools in your toolkit are there to help you move up the ladder, to raise your frequency. Third, energy naturally flows, like a river, unless there is something blocking it. The scale keeps you motivated by showing you the value of transmuting lower vibrating emotions that prevent you from experiencing the joy and love you are seeking. Prevent you from attracting higher vibrating people, opportunities, and experiences. Applying what you learned about the law of attraction, as you evolve, your electromagnetic field will attract more goodness into your life. It really is that simple. Simple but not always easy.

You are now picturing yourself moving up a ladder but that is not the whole picture. A hierarchal image or concept like a ladder does not capture your actual experience. The image that matches your journey is the spiral, the universal concept of growth, transformation and interconnectedness. The spiral is feminine, as much as the ladder is male. It represents life, energy and our ever-evolving journey. It is found in the human body, animals, plants and minerals in nature as well as weather patterns. This imagery suggests that our journey ebbs and flows, with periods of more intense growth and then times of transitional pauses. In the spiral, you can see how energy ebbs and flows.

No matter how strong your practice is and the years you have dedicated yourself to it, you will have unexpected challenges, suddenly grapple-hooked by your past. Whether it's navigating a turbulent relationship, contending with a demanding boss, facing financial setbacks, or experiencing betrayal, these obstacles can feel disheartening, and you may think that you should have moved beyond them by now. However, it's crucial not to lose hope. Instead, consider a different viewpoint.

Quantum physics says that time doesn't move in a straight line but has a cyclical dynamic. That is why you loop back in time to heal something in the past - before you can step into your desired future. In other words, you go back to go forward. You resolve old wounds and limiting beliefs before the future can unfold positively. A past trauma can hold the energy needed for you to take your next step forward.

Paula's Story

I've successfully regained my focus and momentum precisely one more time than I've lost it. I suggest you set that as a strategy.

Let me explain. Some time ago, a life coach helped me identify my archetypes – those clusters of energy that drive and shape our life's journey. I resonated strongly with the maverick archetype, characterized by going against the grain and doing things in my own unique way. Additionally, I recognized traits of the explorer archetype, embodying a curious mind constantly seeking what lies beyond the known. Lastly, I identified with the nurturer archetype, driven by a desire to care for and support others.

Combining these archetypes with shamanic energy medicine has presented its challenges. My maverick nature resisted seeking a mentor, leaving me without guidance at times of need. While my explorer side liked to try new things, enriching my learning experiences, it also meant navigating steep climbs and encountering mixed outcomes. And my nurturing tendencies sometimes led me to assist others without proper discernment, draining my energy and resources.

That combination, left unchecked, culminated in a health crisis in 2016. I was not feeling well, physically, emotionally, mentally nor spiritually. I was depressed, rarely left my home, and my hair was falling out.

I turned to a friend who put me in contact with a shaman with experience extracting dark energies.

We met at Starbucks. She sat down, looked at me and said, *"You have twenty-four dark entities on your field. Go home and pray to St. Michael. You got yourself into this mess, now you need to get yourself out."*

I thought she was arrogant, egotistical and not helpful. I have not changed my opinion. However, I did learn my lesson. In my eagerness to help others, I did not take the necessary precautions to protect myself. Neither was I consistently upgrading my own energy field, as in doing all the practices in this book. A mentor, which I did not have, would have intervened at an earlier stage.

I share this for two reasons. One, there is no way to avoid running into yourself! Who you will find on your journey, always, is yourself. You will want to observe, learn, grow and move on. Our culture is overly committed to punishment, blame, and self-criticism. Spend little to no time in those arenas. Secondly, there is significant value in the slow but sure approach to spiritual growth. In fact, leap frogging up the Scale of Consciousness is an illusion. Build your toolkit as you read our book, add and delete as you go. Remember your journey will ebb and flow, a cyclical process.

Christian psychologist Michael Mangis also describes our personal and spiritual growth as a cyclical process. His analogy may prove helpful to you.

"We can think of spiritual growth not as a linear progression but as a cyclical process. It resembles a journey around a mountain. I come back to the same side of the mountain and see what is essentially the same view, except that now I see it from a different height and with greater clarity. Our growth is cyclical like that. It is not a ladder but a winding staircase. It is not a straight line but more like a helix. We need to purge our house of idols not once but repeatedly throughout our lives."

Reference: **derekdemars.com/2018/05/28/the-spiral-of-spiritual-growth/**

This spiral imagery is also captured in the ancient sacred symbol of the labyrinth, used across cultures for over 4000 years.

Labyrinth aerial view courtesy of Broughton Sanctuary, UK

Your authors have traversed the winding road of personal and spiritual development, and learned valuable lessons along the way that are here in these nine insights aimed at helping you stay focused on your intention and desired long-term outcomes.

1. **Set Firm Boundaries**. Your 'cave time' needs to be respected and given a status of importance for it to remain available to you. Set a schedule that is realistic and wrap the rest of your day around it.

2. **Discover methods to shield yourself from external negative forces.** Explore our webpage for a comprehensive guide detailing 10 effective strategies to safeguard yourself from adverse energies.

3. **Gentle Loving Persistence.** Recognize that your subconscious mind has NO interest in adopting new beliefs. Your toolkit is a threat to humanity as far as it is concerned. Ha!

   For example, you enthusiastically practice the affirmation, life supports me all the time. Your old wiring, the world is a scary place is still persistent for months to come – not because you haven't tried changing it; it takes longer than you expect.

   Be gentle with your underbelly, letting her know that all is well. Gentle loving persistence wins the day.

4. **Find a Mentor.** Mentors are invaluable. Be discerning. It does not need to be a 1-on-1 relationship which can be unaffordable; someone you follow and listen to regularly is a good place to begin.

5. **Like-minded individuals.** It is through the buddy system that everyone wins. Decades of self-efficacy research supports the strong effects of peer support and the belief that *"if you can do it so can I"*. Make sure you have one good non-judgmental listener who shares your values and beliefs. Someone who is a bit further down the road than you.

6. **Shuffle the Deck.** Sometimes you need to do a shuffle and choose new tools or make other changes in your practice. If you are drawn to explore new things, do so. As you grow and expand, your practices need to expand with you.

7. **Spend time in nature.** Make sure nature is highlighted in your toolkit. Being in nature, with all social media turned off, allows you to use all five senses physical and spiritual to experience oneness. Use this tool often to stay on track. You, after all, are a part of nature and nature is a part of you.

8. **Outward Focus.** Generously share your gifts and talents. It is an assured way to raise your vibration and to stay on track. Others need you to show up for them. As you show up for them, you are showing up for yourself. Altruism ranks high on the Scale of Consciousness.

9. **Life is messy, wear an apron.** When you find yourself in a messy situation, they happen, ask yourself, *"Where am I in all this mess?"* What has been my contribution? Your next steps should springboard from the insights you discover.

Sally's Story

January in Florida brought some unusually cold days, and Sally was hesitant to put air in her bike tires. She paid attention to the intuitive sense that flow allowed her, and she worried that she might over-inflate them and that they might explode. She felt she was right not to add the air, but when talking to a friend about her concerns, she was ridiculed.

Her friend, Danny, literally laughed at her and told her that adding air to the tires would not cause them to explode. He said that was a myth and such a thing could never happen.

Sally felt belittled by his reaction and how he treated her. Her confidence in her intuition was shaken and she became upset and kept thinking about her experience with Danny. Relationships often pose the greatest challenges to staying in flow.

Danny inflated his bike tires, after criticizing Sally for being silly for worrying about a tire exploding. He set out for his morning bike ride on a cold morning. To his amazement, one of his bike tires exploded.

With humility, he called Sally and told her about it. They both had a good laugh which mended the tension between them, and Sally not only felt vindicated for listening to the flow of her intuition but also was able to release the residual upsetting emotions that the confrontation had raised.

Leigh's Story

At 55 years of age, I felt very much together in my life. I was the Associate Director of my organization, soon to be the COO and I had a spiritual business on the side. I worked consistently with my daily practices to stay in flow. Always interested in continuing my spiritual exploration and education, I signed up for a workshop with a spiritual guru that was promoted as *"life changing"*. I did not know the content but had heard stories of tremendous transformations from others who went to it. My mother, who had been close to death, died before the workshop.

The first evening of the workshop was a type of primal therapy. There were 20 of us in the group and one by one people got up in the center and *"worked out"* issues with their mothers. They ended up crying or screaming. I was mortified. This was not my type of workshop! I did not feel I had anything to work out with my mother. That night as I got into bed in the hotel room, I thought about leaving the next morning. Suddenly, I sat upright in bed and thought, *"I hate my mother"!*

The next morning, I was the first up in the center of the group, screaming and working through some of my issues with my mother. When the workshop was over, I was traumatized. It was a tremendous shock to learn that I wasn't as together as I thought. I recognized that I had been repressing some trauma from early childhood, even though I thought I had dealt with it. I was a work in progress for a while as I moved toward getting back into the flow of my life.

As these experiences reveal, at any time you might find yourself out of sync with your goal of flow. Living in flow is more than a set of practices and techniques that you grab from your toolkit. It is a process of living life in conscious awareness, a process that can often have you dealing with past events and emotions that come from your earlier life or from your current relationships. That's why the insights provided are so important as a guide for you to follow when you experience a difficult period of ebb and flow.

Don't become discouraged. Give yourself the grace to reset as often as needed. As your commitment ebbs and flows, return always to the practices and the honoring of the path you have chosen.

EXERCISE : Mapping Your Life Journey

Take time with this exercise. Perhaps set aside an afternoon, or several afternoons, where you can work on this uninterrupted. Gather your materials in advance and make some notes of experiences that come to the forefront of your mind at various ages. Most of all, let this exercise be like play. Forget all the rules, create your personal map as feels right to you. There is no one right way. The right way will be your way.

The materials needed are a set (or sets) of colored markers, poster board or large flip-chart paper and a ruler or other straight edge that you can use to make the lines.

Instructions:

1. Begin by setting up your poster board horizontally. Use your straight line-making tool to draw a straight horizontal line across the board from left to right. Now draw a vertical line connected to the horizontal line, forming an L-shape.

2. Label the horizontal axis: Age. Place "0" on the left end and mark your current age on the right end. This horizontal line represents your physical development. Use colored markers to express important physical milestones and events along this timeline. For example, mark growth spurts, injuries, illnesses, puberty, and other significant moments related to your physical body.

3. Now, moving up the vertical axis, draw a line representing your emotional body. Use colored markers to indicate significant emotional experiences, relationships, challenges, and growth points throughout your life.

4. Moving up the vertical axis, the next line represents your mental body. Draw another line, parallel to the physical and emotional timelines, to depict your mental development. Use colored markers to document important intellectual milestones, such as educational achievements, moments of new learning and growth, academic pursuits, and significant insights or realizations.

5. Finally, the top line on the vertical axis represents your spiritual life. Draw a line parallel to the previous timelines to illustrate your spiritual evolution. Use colored markers to capture key religious or spiritual experiences, moments of awakening, growth in consciousness, spiritual practices, and any significant shifts in your beliefs or worldview.

6. Once you've completed mapping out your life journey across the physical, emotional, mental, and spiritual dimensions, take a step back and reflect on the patterns, connections, and insights that emerge from the exercise. Perhaps imagine these four integrated aspects of yourself circling around a mountain making their way up and around. Allow this visual representation to deepen your understanding of your life's story and guide your continued growth and self-discovery.

See your life's journey as a continuous stream rather than a fixed path. There's no such thing as falling off track. Embrace your fallibility with forgiveness, humor and love. Every twist, turn, pause, and restart reflects the richness of your experiences and mirrors your inner growth. Your inner world shapes your outer journey; as you evolve internally, your external circumstances shift accordingly. The tools provided are meant to assist you in transforming your inner landscape, paving the way for a brighter, happier, and more fulfilling life.

Chapter Twelve : A Life in Flow - A Story of Syncronicity

As you work with the concept of 24/7 Flow, you may notice the appearance of synchronicities in your life. That is because the energy of flow is when awareness and experience are synchronized!

What may appear magical or unusual becomes part of the everyday path of living in flow. An astonishing number of multiple synchronicities can occur.

Paula's Story – The Hilton Family and Neurodivergence

I was in the UK on a three-hour train ride, going from the Yorkshire Dales area to London. At one of the stops, a man got on and took a seat next to me. He seemed a bit agitated, and we didn't talk during the ride. However, when we reached London, we somehow discovered that we were both heading to Luton Airport. This meant we had to change trains.

As we moved through London's King's Cross train station, conversation flowed easily between us. We navigated ramps, stairs, an escalator, and a brief walk outside, eventually arriving at St. Pancras International train station, Platform #1. We were ready to catch the 11:15 AM train to

Luton. Being a bit early, we decided to circle back and grab sandwiches and drinks. While waiting for me to checkout, the gentleman looked at his crabmeat sandwich, and reminisced about having the very same sandwich during his short visit to New York City a few years back.

As we strolled and chatted, I learned he had been originally scheduled to take a whole other route to Luton, but that train had been canceled. He shared that he was a farmer and had 3 children. When he asked about my occupation, I explained my interest in science and consciousness, a path I pursued after my daughter's passing and my strong belief that life lives on. By the time we boarded the train to Luton and settled into our seats, our conversation had become livelier. He explained that he was not going to the airport per se, but rather to a meeting at the nearby Hilton Hotel. He was hoping the car he had scoped out on E-bay was all he wanted it to be, as it would be a birthday gift for his wife. Happily, he showed me a photo of his hopeful purchase, a 1974 VW Beetle. Oddly, only a few days prior I had posted on Facebook, a photo of a VW Beetle, with a funny caption; I showed it to him. We agreed that the two cars were the same year and model, one a dirty yellow and the other a recently painted green.

He said that his mother used to practice Reiki, a form of energy healing and then shared that when his daughter was one year's old, she used to stare into space as if she was looking at someone else in the room. He was not surprised to hear about the research describing those kinds of children's experiences. Then he added. "My daughter has autism so that may have influenced things."

Our conversation began to feel more than coincidental. Just as he started explaining the remarkable ways sound is used to aid their daughter who is now 11 years old, the train arrived at the station. Clearly, there was more to share and explore. I asked him to put his information into my contacts.

He looked up and said, *"I don't even know your name."*

"'Paula," I replied.

He typed his name and said, *"My name is Alex. Alex Hilton."*

"Alex was my daughter's name," I shared.

Clearly moved, he finished typing his name.

"Isn't Hilton the name of the hotel you are going to?" I asked, not letting him miss the multiple synchronicities of the day.

"That too. I think this is all a good omen for my car deal," he said with a smile.

A few hours later, Alex sent me a photo of his new car. A few weeks after that initial meeting, I was on a video call with Alex, his wife Cat and daughter Isla. Isla was diagnosed on the autism spectrum when she was young. She was adorable, popping into the video from time to time, sharing her ideas whenever asked. Their other two children have also been diagnosed with autism.

It became immediately obvious how much this family relied on music and sound to get them through their day. In fact, music and sound were the main strategies this family used to handle their challenges, like calming strong emotions during transitions, facing social anxiety, and getting a good night's sleep.

Whenever they moved from home to the car, music was a must. Cat had a collection of favorite songs, which she played to ease her stress throughout the day. Getting Isla to sleep was a bit of a process, but they found that synthesized sounds were helpful. Cat used binaural beats as a sleep aid, letting the sound play all night. This way, if she woke up in the middle of the night, she could easily go back to sleep. On the first floor, there was a constant calming sound – the house fan, like white noise. Even when it wasn't necessary for cooling, they kept it on for its soothing effect.

Alex shared that he had his own social anxieties. Before social events, he listened to calming songs with lyrics. He also had a unique method of shouting football chants to calm down. I shared that all his strong vocalization of sound, activated his vagal nerve which lowered his heart rate, reducing his anxiety, as discussed in Chapter Five.

I left the video call feeling in awe. A month later, I was on a zoom call teaching Cat how to activate her vagus nerve through my on-line course. Alex popped in the call to report that his recent neuro evaluation results indicated that he too was on the autism spectrum. Cat and Alex both felt that the results were accurate and that having that confirmation somehow had created more flow, more ease in everyday life. It's important to recognize that autism is a spectrum, meaning individuals with this condition can have a wide range of strengths, abilities, and characteristics.

The intersection of my trip with Alex and the continuing intersections of the family's needs with my work were not merely coincidental. What allowed these connections was my practice of mindfully and consciously working to stay in flow. As you too continue with the techniques, you'll have your own amazing experiences to share.

Bibliography

Clear, J. (2018). *Atomic habits: An easy & proven way to build good habits & break bad ones.* Avery.

Dyer, W. (1997). *Manifest Your Destiny.*
Harper Collins.

Dyer, W. (2004). *The Power of Intention.*
Hay House.

Dyer, W. (2007). *Change Your Thoughts, Change Your Life.*
Hay House.

Emoto, M. (2005). *The Hidden Messages in Water (Illustrated edition).* Aria Books.

Friedlander, S. (1992). *The Whirling Dervishes: Being an Account of the Sufi Order known as the Mevlevis and its Founder the Poet and Mystic Mevlana Jalalu'ddin Rumi (SUNY series in Islam).*
State University of New York Press.

Goldman, J. (2017). *The 7 Secrets of Sound Healing (Revised edition).*
Hay House.

Goldman, J., & Goldman, A. (2017). *The Humming Effect: Sound Healing for Health and Happiness.* Healing Arts Press.

Hawkes, J. W. (2011). *Cell-Level Healing (Reprint edition).*
Beyond Words.

Hawkins, D. (2014). P*ower vs. Force.*
Hay House.

Hicks, E., & Hicks, J. (2004). *Ask and It Is Given.*
Hay House.

Hicks, E., & Hicks, J. (2006). *The Law of Attraction.*
Hay House.

Hill, N. (1937). *Think and Grow Rich.*
The Ralston Society.

Hillman, J. (1997). *The Soul's Code.*
Bantam

Kapps, L 2020. *Catch Some Rays and Spin Those Chakras.*
Self-published.

Koniver, L. (2020). T*he Earth Prescription: Discover the Healing Power of Nature with Grounding Practices for Every Season.* Reveal Press.

Lightbearers of the World, Unite! (2005).
Summit Publications, Inc.

Merry, P. (2023). *Volution: A Philosophy of Reconnection.*
Ubiquity University.

Morin, A. (2017). *13 Things Mentally Strong People Don't Do: Take Back Your Power, Embrace Change, Face Your Fears, and Train Your Brain for Happiness and Success.* William Morrow.

Nestor, J. (2020). Breath: *The New Science of a Lost Art.* Riverhead Books.

Petry, P. (2020). *A Mother's Courage to Awaken: Hope and Inspiration from My Daughter's Journey in the Afterlife.* Mango.

Petry, P. (2024). *The Conduit to Well-Being: Toning Your Vagus Nerve.* On-line curriculum. paulapetry.com/the-vagus-nerve-course-2/

Power, T.J. (2024). *The DOSE Effect: The New Self-Help Guide for 2024 Teaching You How to Hack Your Mental Health for a Better, Happier Life with Simple Tips and Tricks.* HQ.

Prophet, V. (2016). *Violet Flame.*
Summit Publications, Inc.

Rosenberg, S. (2017). *Accessing the Healing Power of the Vagus Nerve: Self-Help Exercises for Anxiety, Depression, Trauma, and Autism.* North Atlantic Books.

Sha, Z. G. (2006). *Soul Mind Body Medicine.*
New World Library.

Singer, M. A. (2013). *The Untethered Soul: The Journey Beyond Yourself.* New Harbinger.

Sise, A., & Bender, B. (2022). *The Energy of Belief.* Capucia, LLC.

St. Teresa of Avila.(Modern Publication 2007). *The Interior Castle.* Dover Publications.

Tolle, E. (2005). *A New Earth: Awakening to Your Life's Purpose.* Penguin.

Villoldo, A. (2021). T*he Shaman's Book of Living and Dying.* Hampton Roads Publishing.

Vaughan-Lee, J. (Ed.). (2016). *Spiritual Ecology: The Cry of the Earth.* The Golden Sufi Center.

Walker, M. (2017). *Why We Sleep: Unlocking the Power of Sleep and Dreams.* Scribner.

Resources

On-Line Tools:
Your Divine Design and Personality Insights

To truly sync with yourself, reaching the peak of flow, it's crucial to delve into the question: *Who Am I?*

This query leads to an exploration of the intrinsic underlying energies that mold your identity. When we recognize these fundamental forces, the essence of our being becomes clearer, unveiling insights into our soul's direction and purpose.

To help you in this exploration are online assessment tools; ancient wisdom being repackaged. It is important to note that these tools only scratch the surface. For deeper exploration, consider consulting experts in the field and tapping into your own inner wisdom during a shamanic journey or meditation. Below are several divine design tools and a suggested Personality Tool.

Divine Design

Astrological Birth Chart

An astrological birth chart, also known as a natal chart, is a map of the positions of celestial bodies at the time of a person's birth. It's based on the principles of astrology, which suggest that these positions can influence an individual's personality, strengths, weaknesses, life path, and potential future events.

By interpreting the placements of the sun, moon, planets, and other astrological points within the chart, astrologers provide insights into various aspects of a person's life, including relationships, career, health, and personal development.

The purpose of examining one's birth chart is to gain self-awareness, understand patterns and tendencies, and make informed decisions in alignment with cosmic energies.

Find out more: **astrograph.com/horoscopes/**

Numerology Life Path

Numerology is the belief in the mystical significance of numbers and their influence on human life. The Life Path number, derived from a person's birthdate, is a central aspect of numerology. It's believed to represent an individual's life purpose, personality traits, and potential challenges.

Calculating the Life Path involves reducing the birthdate to a single digit or a master number (11, 22, 33) which carries special significance.

Find out more: **numerology.com/articles/your-numerology-chart/ life-path-number-calculator/**

Human Design

Human Design is a system that combines elements of astrology, the I Ching, Kabbalah, and the chakra system, among other influences. It provides a blueprint of a person's energetic makeup, including their conscious and unconscious traits, strengths, and areas for growth. Human Design offers insight into decision-making, relationships, and career paths based on one's unique design type, authority, and profile. It's used for personal development and understanding one's purpose and role in the world.

Find out more: **jovianarchive.com/Human_Design/Types**

Personality Type

Enneagram

The Enneagram has its roots in Sufiism and early Christianity and was constructed in its current form by Oscar Ichazo in the 1950's. It is a personality typing system that describes nine interconnected personality types. It's often used for self-discovery, personal growth, and understanding interpersonal dynamics. Each type has its motivations, fears, and desires, providing insight into behavior and ways to develop healthier patterns.

Find out more:

enneagraminstitute.com/the-traditional-enneagram/

eclecticenergies.com/enneagram/test

24/7 Flow: Thrive Around the Clock
On-Line Resources

To find the below resources please visit: **24-7flow.com**

Guided Audio Experiences

Monroe Institute's Sound Frequency Audio Files

Meditation for Relaxation

Meditation for Future Intentions

Shamanic Sacred Garden Journey

Vocal Toning

Self-Assessment Tool

The Joyful Living Assessment